Schofie

English

Key Stage 2

Revision Guide

Carol Matchett

Introduction

The purpose of this book

This book will help you to revise for the English tests at the end of Year 6 and to get better marks in them.

What you will need

Paper and a pencil or pen.

How to use this book

- It is best to start at the beginning and work through each topic in turn. If you prefer, you could use the Contents list or the Index to choose a topic.
- Turn to the topic and read the explanation.
- Some of the words in some topics appear in orange. Their definitions are given in the Glossary on pages 94 and 95. Try to remember them.
- Some of the words in the examples given appear in different colours. Match the coloured words to the coloured notes which appear in boxes beside them. These notes point out important features.
- The **Remember** section at the end of the topic lists the most important things you need to know. Use the **Remember** box as a quick reminder of the main points.
- Try the **Test yourself!** questions. Write your answers on a piece of paper. Then check them against the correct or suggested answers on pages 87 to 91. For some of the questions there is more than one 'correct' answer: it depends on what you decide to write. For questions like these, an example is given of one possible answer. Check whether your answer is similar.
- Maybe you got some questions wrong, or perhaps you're not sure that you understand the topic? Read it again and have another go at the questions.
- If you are happy with your answer and are sure that you understand, tick the circle in the corner of the page, and move on.
- When you have worked through the whole book, check whether there is a tick on every page. Are any circles empty? If so, do you need to go back to those topics and work through them again?
- Read the 'Tips for tests' at the back of this book. Then you are ready to take the tests. Good luck!

How to get even better marks!

Work through the Schofield & Sims English Practice Papers for Key Stage 2, available separately.

Note for teachers and parents

The Schofield & Sims Revision Guides have been written by teachers, for use at school and at home. The Guides enable children to revise independently for the National Curriculum Key Stage tests (SATs). The focus is on clear explanations of the topics covered by the tests, all of which will already have been taught in school. Each English topic is matched to the National Literacy Strategy (NLS), and all the NLS links are listed in the Curriculum chart on pages 92 to 93. Practice Papers designed to accompany this book will further improve children's test results (see back cover for full details).

Contents

How to read a story

Reading a story seems straightforward – you start at the beginning of the book and read to the end. However, **real** reading is much more than this. Let's explore what real reading involves.

Reading is thinking about the story

When you read a story:

- **think about it** – focus on the characters, the events, and how you feel about them
- **make predictions** – about what will happen next (and read on to find out if you are right!)
- **picture it in your head** – try to 'see' all the events, the characters and the settings as they are described.

Thinking like this as you read a story will help you to discuss it or to answer questions about it later.

Reading is asking yourself questions

Real reading involves asking yourself questions as you read. Here are some examples of the kinds of questions that you might ask yourself.

> Why did he or she do that?

> What do I think will happen next?

> What usually happens in stories like this?

> How will the story end?

> Can I picture this character? What words helped me to do this?

> Can I picture this setting? What words helped me to do this?

> Can I picture this event? What words helped me to do this?

> What feelings do I have? Why do I feel like that?

> What parts of the story did I like best? Why?

Don't worry if there are a few words in the story that you do not understand. It is more important to ask yourself questions and to think about the overall meaning of the story.

Test yourself!

Set up a reading log, where you can write down your thoughts and feelings about a story as you read it.

Remember

While you are reading a story, **think** about it.

Ask yourself questions.

Following the plot

The **plot** of a story is the **sequence of events** that takes place. When you are reading, try to keep track of the **main events**, for example, notice what happens in each paragraph of a short story, or in each chapter of a longer story or novel. This will help you to remember the **order** in which events happened and to see **how** the events **link together**. Knowing **when** each event happened is also useful if you are later asked a question about the story. You will be able to quickly go back and find the part of the story that you need to refer to.

Here are some examples of important parts of a story. Look out for them when you are reading.

A starting event

This is usually near the **beginning** of the story. Something happens that sets off the chain of events that follows.

For example, in *Treasure Island* by Robert Louis Stevenson, a mysterious pirate arrives at the Admiral Benbow inn. This event starts off an exciting adventure as the characters go searching for buried treasure.

Conflicts and complications

These are found in the **middle** of stories. Important decisions have to be made, things go wrong and events become more complicated.

For example, in *The Sheep Pig* by Dick King-Smith, a young pig called Babe faces all sorts of problems and complications while trying to fulfil his ambition to become a sheep pig.

The climax of the story

This is the moment of decision, the moment when all issues in the story have to be decided. It usually happens towards the **end** of the story.

For example, in *Krindlekrax* by Philip Ridley, the climax of the story comes when the main character, Ruskin, faces up to Krindlekrax, the monster in the sewers.

The resolution

This happens towards the **end** of the story. It is the moment when the problems and puzzles of the story are finally solved.

For example, in mystery stories the clues all come together and the guilty person is found out.

Test yourself!

Here are the main events in the story *Jack and the Beanstalk*. Number these events in the order they happened, starting with 1:

Jack climbs a beanstalk
Jack steals a magic hen
Jack exchanges his cow for beans
Jack chops down the beanstalk
Jack discovers a castle

Remember

Don't lose the plot! **Keep track of the main events** as you read.

Characters

Characters are vital to a story. As you read a story, you learn more about the characters and you decide what you think about them. Some characters you like, some you dislike. Sometimes you might change your opinion of a character because of something that happens in the story.

Authors create characters through the details they give about them. Look out for these details. They will help you to make decisions about characters. When you read a story, look for clues in: how the characters are described, their actions (how they behave) and the dialogue (what they say).

Creating characters

Using description

Look at how an author uses **description** to introduce a character. Although the words describe the appearance of the character, they also suggest something about the kind of person he is:

A face appeared over the wall: a mop of sunny yellow hair, followed by two twinkling blue eyes, and a cheeky grin...

> These words suggest that the character is friendly and fun

Using actions

In the next example, it is the **actions** of the character that tell us what she is like:

Ellie seemed to deliberately ignore the new girl. She would turn her face away with an indignant flick of her hair and giggle loudly with her friends.

> Ellie's actions suggest that she is trying to make the new girl feel uncomfortable by not including her

Using dialogue

Now look at how **dialogue** can give clues about characters and the relationships between them:

What are you doing here?' he asked accusingly.
'I can come here if I like,' I replied, trying to sound calm.
'But what if I don't like,' he said giving me a cold stare...

> These words and phrases suggest a tension between the two characters. One character seems more powerful

---

Test yourself!

Read this story extract:

Mrs Pringle was like a pillow – soft, comfortable and always there when needed. The Gibson children called her Granny Pringle, although she was no relation to them. But in times of trouble she was always there with her gentle words, cheery smile and delicious biscuits.

Mrs Pringle is kind and friendly. How does the author show this? Find four details used to create this impression.

Remember

Look for details in how characters are **described**, in their **actions** and in **dialogue**.

Characters

Feelings and motives

Responding to characters also means thinking about their feelings and understanding the reasons why they do things (their **motives**). Sometimes the author will tell you this information directly, but more often it is inferred or suggested in the way a character behaves and how events are described. To infer means to draw out ideas from the information given.

As you read a story, look for clues about the feelings of characters. Ask yourself **why** characters behave as they do. Remember, the clues are always in the story so you must refer to the text when discussing feelings and motives.

Direct description

Here, the author tells us directly the feelings of the character and the reason for this:

> Joe was feeling sad. All his friends had gone off without him and he was left all alone…

Not telling but showing

In the next example, rather than **telling** us, the author **shows** us Joe's feelings in his behaviour. Here you have to look for the clues that suggest Joe is feeling upset at being left behind:

Joe's behaviour suggests his feelings

> Joe slumped in a chair, his shoulders hunched. He defiantly pulled his cap down over his eyes and muttered to the empty room, 'Well, I don't care. I didn't want to go anyway.'

The reason why he feels fed up: he might say he doesn't care, but his behaviour suggests that this is not true

Mixed feelings

Feelings aren't always straightforward. Sometimes characters have a mixture of feelings, and authors need to show this:

Signs of nervousness

> Breathing unsteadily, Nick sat on the very edge of his bed. He looked down at the envelope held between his trembling fingers. He turned it over. It was not properly sealed. It would be easy to open. He could quite easily read the contents and then put it back without any one knowing. His face began to burn…

Uncertain whether to open the letter or not… trying to convince himself…

Test yourself!

Read the passage below. Explain fully what it shows about the character's feelings. Refer to words and phrases in the text that lead you to think this.

> Although he walked as slowly as he could, he still came to the gate all too quickly. He looked around, hoping for something to distract him from lifting the catch and walking up the overgrown path. There was nothing. He felt a cold fist clench in his stomach…

Remember

Look for clues that suggest the feelings and motives of characters.

The fiction author's methods

As you are reading, you will notice that some parts of a story are **particularly effective**, for example, moments of **excitement**, **tension**, **suspense**, **mystery** or **surprise**. These are the parts of the story that make us really want to keep reading.

When you find a really gripping part of a story, ask yourself the question: **'How did the author make that work?'** Read that part of the story again. Read it aloud in your head so that you can hear the sound of the text. The methods that authors use to make their writing work well are called techniques. Listen and look for the different techniques that authors use to help their text to work well.

Here are some examples of techniques to look out for.

Creating suspense and tension

Here is an example where the writer is creating suspense and tension. The techniques used have been marked round the outside of the text:

> Description of details

> Questions that make us wonder

He stepped on to the landing, closing the door behind him. He stood in complete darkness, listening. Would he be able to find the way in the dark? What if someone heard him? His heart began to beat faster. He took a long, slow breath. And another. Slowly, he felt his way past the first door, where his brother was sleeping; past the second door, where he could hear his father snoring. Now he felt the handle of the third door...

> Showing feelings

> Delaying and slowing events down

> Building up; repeating a pattern

Creating a sense of panic

In this example, the author uses techniques that create a sense of panic.

> Exclamations

> Verbs suggest panic

The wolves were close behind! Scrambling madly through the trees, the branches catching in her hair, she fought on. Struggling. Stumbling. Desperate. Not daring to look round, knowing they were behind her. Hearing their howls. Feeling the thud of their paws...

> Vivid description of sounds and feelings

> Short sentences for impact and to create sense of pace

Test yourself!

Read this passage. How does the author build up the sense of mystery about the box?

On the dressing table, half-hidden behind a vase of wilting roses, was a small box. It was just a simple wooden box, but something about it seemed to draw him towards it. He picked it up. It was surprisingly heavy. Perhaps there was something inside.

Remember

Don't just say that a story was effective. Ask yourself: 'How did the author make it effective?'

The fiction author's point of view

Stories can be told from different points of view. A story might be written in the **first person**, as if from the point of view of one of the characters. This means that you see the events and other **characters** through this person's eyes.

On the other hand, a story might be written in the **third person**, as if someone is watching and describing the events. However, even in a third person narration we often still see the events from the point of view of one of the characters.

Point of view is important because it affects your **view of the events** and your **response to the characters**.

Some examples of different points of view are described below. See how they affect the reader's response.

Remember

The **point of view** from which a story is told will **affect your view** of the events.

First person narration

This extract is from a story told in the first person. The first person ('I') is the narrator:

> Told from the point of view of one particular member of the class: we see his thoughts, his views, his opinions...

I don't know what it was about Rashid, but he always seemed different to the other lads. Not strange, because he still liked the same things as the rest of us... but just different. The others didn't have much time for him. They would soon tire of his crazy ideas. But not me, I found them enthralling...

> The style is quite informal to fit with the character of the narrator

> A personal view: the others might have described Rashid very differently...

> The effect is to make the reader also want to know more about Rashid

Third person narration

The next example is from a story told in the third person, but again the events are seen from the point of view of one particular character:

> Told from the point of view of Ellie.
> It is her version of the events, her thoughts

Ellie could hear them laughing and giggling in the cloakroom. She did not dare to go in and face their sly smiles and knowing looks.

> This is what Ellie **thinks** is happening. The event might appear totally different if we saw it from **inside** the cloakroom

Test yourself!

Read this extract from the story *Cinderella and her Sisters*. What do you notice about the point of view from which the story is told? How is this different to other versions of the story?

That Cinderella, I never did trust her. She goes around telling all sorts of lies about my sister and I. Just because she is so pretty, she gets away with everything...

The fiction author's choice of language

Words are the most important tools a writer has, so you know that the words used in any story have been **carefully chosen** for their effect. Words can suggest **feelings and moods**, as well as describe **how things look or sound**.

Thinking about words

When you are reading a story, think about words and phrases that you find particularly effective. Ask yourself **why** those words have been chosen. Don't just think about the **meaning** of the word – think also about what it **suggests** in relation to the events in the story. Remember that some words **have more than one meaning** – this might be why the author has chosen them. The examples below will help you to become more aware of how an author chooses which words to use.

A word chosen for more than one reason

She stepped out into the cold night.

The word 'cold' tells us about the temperature outside, but the writer has also chosen the word because it suggests that something unpleasant, chilling, cruel might be waiting in the night. The effect is to make us worry about the person who is about to step outside.

> **Test yourself!**
>
> …The prisoner lay on the stone floor in near darkness, staring up at the precious rectangle of blue sky, high above and out of reach.
>
> Why has the word 'precious' been used to describe the prisoner's view of the sky through the window?

Adjectives that suggest facts

In this example, each adjective chosen helps to suggest that the family being described are poor, rather than stating this fact openly:

The family sat around the simple wooden table. A feeble light came from the small fire that father had built in the grate. Strange shadows were cast on the bare walls…

The use of powerful verbs

In this next example it is the choice of verbs that is important. Each powerful verb chosen helps to suggest a sense of panic:

People poured into the streets. Scrambling over each other in their haste to escape, jostling and pushing. Some were struggling with belongings; others were straining to stay with their families.

> **Remember**
>
> Think about the **choice of words and what they suggest** in relation to that moment in the story.

The fiction author's choice of language

Figurative language in fiction

Sometimes authors use figurative language. This means that they describe **one thing** in terms of **something else**. These comparisons are not supposed to be taken literally. Instead, they create a 'thought picture', which suggests something to the reader. This might be a special feature of the item being described, or a feeling or mood.

Why has figurative language been used?

Look out for examples of figurative language in your own reading, as well as in the examples below. Think about why the author has chosen to use that particular image. Think about the features or ideas that the image suggests, and what it makes you think about. How does this link to the events in the story?

Simile

In this example, a simile is used to suggest the special qualities of a character's voice:

She had a <u>voice like velvet</u>.

Velvet is smooth and soft and rich. These are the special qualities of the voice that are suggested by using this simile.

Here is another simile. This time, it is used to suggest how someone moves:

The man was <u>like a panther stalking its prey</u>.

This simile suggests that the man **does not want to be seen** – he is moving softly, silently, stealthily, but with a definite purpose. The comparison to a 'panther stalking its prey' also suggests that the man is **dangerous**.

Metaphor

Here is a metaphor describing a fire. The metaphor works on more than one level:

The flames were tussling tigers pawing at the sky.

The idea of **tussling tigers** suggests the fierceness and danger in the flames	The word **tigers** suggests the colour of the flames	The idea of pawing tigers suggests the movements of the flames reaching up into the sky

Test yourself!

Underline the simile used in this extract. Why did the author choose to describe the cave in this way?

The children spent every day of their holiday on the beach and the cave was like a magnet to them. They loved to explore the echoing chamber...

Remember

Think about the **features, qualities or feelings** suggested by a **simile** or **metaphor**.

Genre – type of story

Genre is a word used to describe **different types of writing**, for example, **fantasy, adventure, romance** or **horror**. Each genre has its own special features, such as typical characters, settings, events, themes or language. As you read a story, look out for familiar features and think about how you would describe the story to a friend.

Knowing the genre sometimes helps you to predict how a story will end. But remember, writers will sometimes play around with these ideas and surprise us by introducing something completely different and unexpected.

Here are some examples of features found in different story genres.

Clues to the genre

In this folk tale, the genre is clear from the opening:

Typical opening – events often happened long ago	Typical characters/ stereotypes	Theme of rich and poor

Long ago there lived a poor farmer. He lived with his wife in a little stone farmhouse at the edge of the fields. One day the farmer was hard at work in his fields when an old man came by. The old man doffed his hat to the farmer and said: 'Good morning, young man! How would you like to be rich?' Well, as you can imagine the farmer was very surprised at this…

Setting	The voice of the story teller	Possible magical event to follow

Even the title of a story can suggest the genre and lead you to expect a certain type of story:

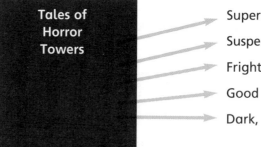

Tales of Horror Towers

- Supernatural or evil forces
- Suspense, uncertainty
- Frightening events, danger
- Good against evil
- Dark, creepy settings

Test yourself!

A book is described as an **adventure story**.

What features would you expect to find in an adventure story? Think about:

- the characters
- the events
- how the story might end.

Remember

Look for **familiar features** in stories. But also remember that **not all stories** fit neatly into **one genre**.

Themes and messages

The **theme** of a story is the main idea that runs through it. Some examples of typical story themes would be the struggle between good and evil, or dealing with a particular problem. Sometimes the theme is developed into a **message** for the reader. This is particularly true in traditional stories.

When you are thinking about story themes and messages, **take a step back** and think about the **whole story** and the **overall idea** behind it. Sometimes themes and messages are clearly stated by the author through comments. At other times, themes and messages are only suggested through the events of the story.

Clearly stated themes

Here is an example where the theme of the story is clearly introduced by the author with the opening sentence. The story begins:

Secrets can be dangerous things…

The rest of the story is about someone with a secret and the problems it causes. Comments like this at the start or end of a story help to identify the theme or message.

Clues in the title

Titles can also be useful in identifying themes. For example, a collection of short stories might have the title:

Happy Families?

A collection of short stories

This title suggests that all of the stories will be about families. The question mark suggests that at least some of the stories might be about problems that occur within families

Clearly stated messages

The message of a story can be clearly stated. For example, a **fable** often ends with a moral such as:

Slow and steady wins the day.

Themes and messages suggested by events

More often, both messages and themes are suggested by the events that take place or what happens to the characters. For example, in the story with the message: 'Slow and steady wins the day', a slow, steady character overcomes all the odds to defeat a faster but less reliable opponent.

Test yourself!

Here is an outline of a traditional story:

Two hungry brothers find a chapatti lying on a stone. They argue about who found it and who should eat it. A stranger appears and says he will help them divide the chapatti in two so that they can share it. However, the stranger tricks them and ends up eating all of the chapatti himself – the two brothers are left with nothing.

What is the message of this story? Explain your answer by referring to events in the story.

Remember

Themes and messages can be clearly stated by the author, or suggested by the events of the story.

Illustrations in fiction

Stories are often accompanied by **illustrations** (pictures). In some cases, the illustrations are **added to a story** that has already been written. Although the story makes sense without the illustrations, the pictures help you to visualise or see the events, or to capture the mood or atmosphere of the story.

In other stories, the pictures are **central to the telling of the story** – for example, in picture books or comic strips. When reading stories like these, you have to 'read' the pictures as well as the text. It is rather like watching a film or a television programme where the sound and pictures are equally important.

Below you can read more about the different ways in which illustrations are used.

Test yourself!

You have been asked to illustrate a book called *Tales of Horror Towers*.

What sort of illustration do you think would best suit the stories in this book?

Illustrations that help you to visualise the story

As suggested above, illustrations might be added to an existing story to help you visualise the events, characters or settings. This can be particularly helpful if the setting is an unfamiliar one such as a fantasy world or a historical setting.

Illustrations that help you to feel the mood of the story

The style of illustration and the colours used can add to the mood or atmosphere of a story. For example:

- soft pastel colours – old-fashioned, warm-hearted, pleasant, dream-like
- heavy dark colours – sinister, threatening.

Remember

Illustrations can be used in different ways. Think about what the illustrations add to the story.

Illustrations that are central to the story

In a comic strip, the illustrations are central to the story. They replace most of the description and narrative needed in a normal story.

There is no need to describe what is happening because it is shown in the picture.

Responding to fiction

It is important to develop your own opinion about the books you read. This means being able to describe what you thought about a story and comment on what you found effective.

If you are asked for your opinion, there is **no right or wrong answer**. Everyone has their own opinion. However, you must explain your ideas by referring to different features of the book and giving examples. Think what you liked or disliked about a book, then ask yourself the important question: why? Why was the story exciting/interesting/realistic…? Why did it fail to grip me? The example below is one example of a personal response.

You can read about responding to poems on page 17 and responding to non-fiction on page 33.

Personal response to the story
Abby's Abominable Adventure

A general comment is backed up by an example from the story

Comments on the plot

The story was really exciting, particularly when Abby was trapped and it seemed she would not escape. I liked how the author built up the suspense by describing all the little sounds and used questions to show what Abby was thinking.

The ending was a real surprise because it was Mikey who helped her escape and all along he had seemed to be her enemy. Abby had been wrong about him all the time…

Comments on techniques used by the author

Comments on characters and the author's use of surprise

Giving your opinion – some hints

Supporting your opinions

To help you support your opinions, use phrases that give reasons and examples. For example:

I thought it was ___ when…
I liked the part where ___ because…
It was really ____, for example when…
I liked how the author___ by/because…

Dealing with mixed feelings

You might have mixed feelings about a book. There might be some aspects that you like, and other parts that you felt did not really work. This is fine. Just explain what you thought worked well and what you disliked.

Test yourself!

Think about a story that you have read recently. Did you enjoy reading the story? Explain your opinion by referring to different aspects of the story.

Remember

Always give reasons and examples to support your opinions.

Reading poems

There are many different types of poetry. Poems can be quite short, but they often have a lot to say. You can read a poem over and over again and each time notice something new and interesting.

When you first read a poem, read it aloud in your head so that you can hear the sound of the words. Think about how the poem makes you feel and what it makes you think about. These are your **first impressions** of the poem. Later you can go back and read the poem again, noticing how and why the poem worked.

Here is an example of things you might think about when you are reading a poem.

This poem is called 'The Sands of Dee' and is by Charles Kingsley. Try reading the poem aloud in your head.

What do you picture as you read each part of the poem?

How does the poem make you feel? How would you describe the mood of the poem?

What parts of the poem (lines, phrases) stand out?

What does the poem make you think about?

The Sands of Dee

'O Mary, go and call the cattle home,
　　And call the cattle home,
　　And call the cattle home,
　　Across the sands of Dee';
The western wind was wild and dank with foam,
And all alone went she.

The western tide crept up along the sand,
　　And o'er and o'er the sand,
　　And round and round the sand,
　　As far as eye could see.
The rolling mist came down and hid the land:
　　And never home came she.

'O is it weed, or fish, or floating hair –
　　A tress of golden hair,
　　A drowned maiden's hair,
　　Above the nets at sea?'
Was never salmon yet that shone so fair
　　Among the stakes on Dee.

They rowed her in across the rolling foam,
　　The cruel crawling foam,
　　The cruel hungry foam,
　　To her grave beside the sea:
But still the boatmen hear her call the cattle home
　　Across the sands of Dee.

Test yourself!

Write down your first thoughts and feelings after reading this poem.

Remember

Read a poem aloud in your head. Think about **how the poem makes you feel** and what **pictures** it creates.

Responding to poems

Some poems create a strong picture in your mind. Some poems create feelings and moods. Other poems have a theme or message that makes you think about the subject.

When thinking about poems, it is important that you can explain **what it is** about the poem that makes you think or feel as you do. Read again the poem 'The Sands of Dee'. This time, look for particular parts of the poem that made you respond in this way. You can refer to these parts of the poem when discussing your ideas about the poem.

The comments below show how you might refer to particular parts of verses one and two when explaining your thoughts and ideas. Read the comments. Then consider what you would say about some of the language and content of verses three and four.

These lines make you worry about the girl because the weather and sea sound so unpleasant ('wild and dank') and the girl is all by herself ('And all alone went she.')

This verse of the poem builds up to the last line by describing how the tide slowly covers the sand and the mists come down. Then in the last line we are told that the girl never came home.

Test yourself!

In the **last verse** of the poem 'The Sands of Dee', which lines remind you that the sea was responsible for the girl's death?

Remember

Support your ideas about a poem by saying what **lines, words or phrases** made you think that.

The poet's choice of language

Poets choose words very carefully. Every word in a poem adds to the overall impact. Look out for words and phrases that you find particularly effective and think about **why** the poet chose those words.

Remember that the choice of words is always linked to what the poet is trying to say or put across in the poem. The poet might be describing **exactly** what things look, sound or feel like. He or she could be **creating a mood or feeling** – or suggesting **many ideas** through just one word.

Words that suggest feelings and mood

Below you will find some examples of how words and phrases are chosen to suggest feelings and mood as well as to describe how something looks, sounds or feels.

Suggesting a mood

In the poem 'The Sands of Dee', we are told that:

> The western wind was wild and dank with foam,

The words 'wild' and 'dank' are used to describe the scene (it was blustery and damp) but they also help to create a dark and threatening mood. (The word 'wild' might also have been chosen for the sound it makes alongside the words 'western' and 'wind'.)

Describing movements and feelings

Here is an extract from the poem 'The Cataract of Lodore' by Robert Southey. (A cataract is a waterfall.) Look at the words chosen to describe the water:

> The poet has chosen lots of powerful verbs that suggest the different movements of the water

> The cataract strong then plunges along;
> Striking and raging as if a war waging
> Its caverns and rocks among;
> Rising and leaping, sinking and creeping,
> Swelling and sweeping, showering and springing
> Flying and flinging, writhing and wringing...

> This long list of verbs helps to suggest the rushing speed of the water. There are no pauses

> Lots of the verbs suggest sudden, fast, wild movements

Test yourself!

In the poem 'The Eagle', the poet (Alfred Lord Tennyson) describes an eagle sitting on a cliff top looking down at the sea. He writes:

> The wrinkled sea beneath him crawls

Why do you think the poet used the word 'wrinkled' to describe the sea?

Remember

Think about what a particular word or phrase suggests to you as it is used in the poem.

The poet's choice of language

Figurative language in poetry

Poets often use figurative language to help them create pictures (images), express moods and suggest ideas. For example, they might use:

- a simile or metaphor to compare the thing they are describing with something else
- personification to describe an object or idea as if it were a human being.

Look out for examples of these techniques in poems you read. Think about why the poet chose to make the comparison. What particular feature or quality was the poet trying to suggest? As you read the examples below, remember that figurative language is a **powerful tool** because it can suggest a number of different ideas.

Simile

First, a simile found in the extract from 'The Cataract of Lodore' on page 18:

> The cataract strong then plunges along;
> Striking and raging as if a war waging

This is a simile because it uses the word **as** to make a direct comparison between the waterfall and a war. (The word **like** is sometimes used in similes)

The simile helps to put across the sound and fury of the water

Metaphor

Here, another poet uses a series of metaphors to describe a storm:

> Lightning, an angry scar across the dark sky,
> Thunder, a threatening voice calling from on high,
> Rain, a shower of glassy splinters hurtling down, ...

As well as describing what the scene looked like, the metaphors also help to create a dark and threatening mood

Personification

Here is an example of **personification** taken from the poem 'Shadow March' by Robert Louis Stevenson. In this poem the shadow is described as if it were human:

> All round the house is the jet black night
> It stares through the window pane

Test yourself!

In the poem 'The Eagle' the poet ends with the lines:

He watches from his
    mountain walls,
And like a thunderbolt
    he falls.

Why do you think the poet compares the eagle to a thunderbolt?

Remember

Think about **what is suggested** by a simile, metaphor or personification.

Sound patterns

Poets don't only choose words for their meaning, but also for the **sound patterns** they can make. This is why it is important to always read poems aloud in your head. You should listen for sound patterns such as:

• rhyme   • rhythm   • alliteration   • onomatopoeia.

Listen to the effect and think about **why** the poet wants the poem to sound like this.

Here are some examples of different sound patterns found in poems.

Rhythm and rhyme

First some lines with a strong rhythm and rhyme. They are taken from the poem 'From a railway carriage', by Robert Louis Stevenson:

> Faster than fairies, faster than witches,
> Bridges and houses, hedges and ditches;
> And charging along like troops in a battle,
> All through the meadows the horses and cattle...

Rhyming couplets (pairs of rhyming lines)

In this poem, the strong, fast rhythm sounds like the noise of the train hurrying along the track. The rhyme adds to the rhythm and helps the poem hurry along

Alliteration

Here are some examples of lines using **alliteration**:

> The soft whisper of sea on sand

The repeated letter 's' creates a soft, whispering sound

> The wild wind whipped the waves in fury

The repeated 'w' sound is very strong. It sounds like the wild, whipping sound of the wind

Onomatopoeia

Here is an example of a short poem using lots of **onomatopoeia**:

> Slip, slop, slosh
> Waves round my legs
> Slop, splosh, splish
> Waves retreat again

Onomatopoeia is used to describe the sound of the water. The words sound fun and help to make it a fun poem

Test yourself!

Here is the first part of the poem 'The Eagle':

> He clasps the crag with
>   crooked hands;
> Close to the sun in
>   lonely lands,
> Ring'd with the azure
>   world, he stands.

What sound patterns does the poet use in this part of the poem? Give examples.

Remember

Read the poem **aloud in your head**. Listen for **sound patterns** and think about **how they make the poem sound**.

Poem structure and form

The **form** of a poem is its shape and structure. There are many different forms of poetry. Sometimes poems are written to a very **strict structure**, such as a particular **rhyme pattern** or **number of syllables**. Other forms of poem allow the poet more choice.

Think about why the poet has chosen a particular form and how he or she has fitted the ideas into that form. Some poem forms are usually used for humorous poems, while others are usually descriptive. As you read the examples below, think about the different effects.

Haiku

These are usually descriptive poems. They are very short and focus on a single image or detail. A haiku has a very strict structure. It is three lines long and each line must have the correct number of syllables – 5, 7, 5.

> Water, calm and still;
> Dragonflies hovering, not
> Touching the surface.

Kenning

Kennings are also descriptive. But a kenning describes something without saying what it is. A poem can be made up of a list of phrases describing the same subject. For example:

> Heat generator
> Sweat maker
> Skin burner
> Water stealer

In this case, each line describes the sun

Limerick

These are humorous poems with a very strict rhythm and rhyme. A limerick is only five lines long. Here is an example of a limerick:

> There once was a dog known as Fred
> Who wouldn't get out of his bed.
> He said: 'There's no way!
> I'll stay here all day –
> Until I desire to be fed.'

Test yourself!

Read the limerick about the dog called Fred.

What do you notice about the rhythm and rhyme of the poem?

Remember

Poets choose the form of their poem as well as the subject of their poem.

Writing a commentary

A **commentary** is a formal way of explaining your ideas and understanding of a poem or a story. The idea of a commentary is to **draw attention to particular features or parts of the text** and to comment on them. For example, a commentary might explain what the poet or author says, or comment on features such as the writer's use of language.

In a commentary, you are expected to refer to particular parts of the poem or story. This includes using direct quotations taken from the text.

Writing a commentary – some hints

Here are some ideas to help you write a commentary on a poem. Most of these ideas could also be used for a commentary on a story.

Refer to the text

Make sure that you refer to particular parts of the poem to explain your ideas. Use phrases like:

The poet says that…
When the poet writes… he/she means…
In the poem it says…
At the start of the poem…
In the last verse…

Use quotations

Use a quotation from the actual poem to back up your ideas. A quotation means copying the exact words from the text and putting them in speech marks, as in these examples:

The poet makes the poem hurry along. The following lines are a good example of this:

*'Faster than fairies, faster than witches,
Bridges and houses, hedges and ditches;'*

The poet does not seem to like the sun that much because it is described as a 'skin burner' and a 'water stealer'.

> The speech marks show that these words or lines are taken directly from the poem

Explain the poet's methods

In a commentary on a poem you might explain:

- what the poet is trying to say in the poem
- the poet's choice of words or use of imagery
- the structure or sound patterns in the poem
- the mood of the poem.

Test yourself!

Water, calm and still;
Dragonflies hovering, not
Touching the surface.

Use a quotation to back up the following comment about this haiku:

The scene sounds very peaceful…

Remember

Use quotations to back up your comments. Put the quotations in speech marks.

Reading non-fiction

We sometimes read non-fiction texts to find a particular **fact** or the answer to a specific question. On other occasions, we might read the whole article or book and then think about the information it gave us.

In both cases, it is a good idea to **skim** the text before you read it properly. Skimming gives you an idea of **what the text is about**, **what aspects of the subject are covered** and **how the information is organised**. As you read, notice details about information given in each part of the text. This skim read will be useful if you need to go back to the text later to check particular pieces of information.

What to look out for as you skim – some hints

The main heading/s

Headings tell you what the text is about. The heading might also give you a clue about the purpose of the text, for example:

How to build an aquarium

The fascinating world of frogs

> Gives you instructions for building an aquarium

> Gives you information about frogs

Sub-headings

Sub-headings give you a clue about the main ideas in the text. They can also show you how the text is organised. For example, imagine these were the sub-headings in an article on motor cars:

Horseless carriages: the first motorcars
The start of mass production
The golden age of motoring
Designs today: speed, comfort and convenience
The future of motoring

> These sub-headings show that the information is organised in chronological or time order. The text is likely to recount the history and development of the motor car, rather than describing the different parts of cars or explaining how they work

Test yourself!

If you have not already done so, skim through this book.

What do you notice about the subject matter and how the information is organised?

Which parts of the book did you look at to help you with this task?

Diagrams, illustrations and captions

A quick glance at illustrations is useful to give you an idea of the subject matter of a text. But it is important to go back and read with care any captions and labels accompanying the illustrations.

Remember

Skim the text quickly before you read it. Look for headings and the main ideas.

Finding information

Skimming and **reading through** a text gives you a good overview of the information given. You will know where to look if you need to go back and find a particular piece of information quickly.

Identifying key words and **scanning** will also help you to find the information you need without reading vast chunks of text. Scan the page or section where the information is likely to be found, looking for the key word. When you find the key word read that part of the text carefully. If that part of the text does not give the answer try scanning again.

Here is a question that asks you to find some information.

> What are the two main differences between the inner planets and the outer planets? Scan this information to find the answer.

This is the information needed	These are the key words you need to **scan** for. Scan the text now to find these key words

The solar system

The solar system is made up of the Sun, the planets that orbit the Sun and other bodies such as moons, comets and meteorites.

At the moment there are nine planets known to orbit the Sun. Astronomers believe that there may be a tenth planet still to be discovered.

The inner planets, those closest to the Sun, are small and rocky. They include Mercury, Venus, Earth and Mars. Most of the outer planets, such as Jupiter, Saturn, Uranus and Neptune, are huge giants made from gases and liquids. **Pluto, the furthest known planet from the Sun, is rocky, but icy. It takes Pluto 248 years to orbit the Sun.**

Mercury, the closest planet to the Sun, is also the smallest. It orbits the Sun once every 88 days. Jupiter, the fifth planet from the Sun, is the largest in the Solar System.

> Scanning for the key words helps you to find the relevant part of the text quickly. Read these sentences carefully to find the answer

Answer: The inner planets are small and rocky. The outer planets are huge and are made from gas and liquid.

Test yourself!

Scan the information about the Solar System to quickly find the answer to these questions. The key words in the questions are in bold.

What is the name of the **fifth planet** from the sun?

What words describe the surface of the planet **Pluto**?

Remember

Identify key words in the question. **Scan** the text to find these words. Read that part carefully.

Finding information

Gathering and presenting information

Sometimes you need to gather information from **different places** and present it in a given format, such as an **information table** or a **diagram**.

Taking time to identify the key words and scan the text will still help you to find the relevant information. But you should not expect to find all of the information **in one place**. Make sure you know the information you need, and then scan the text to find each piece of information until you have completed the task.

Making notes on the planets in the Solar System

Here is an example of a note-making or summary table that could be completed using the information about the Solar System on page 24.

> The names of the planets are the key words to scan for in the text

> The headings tell you the information required about each planet

Planet	Position	Description	Orbit
Mercury			
Earth	3rd from the Sun	Small and rocky	$365\frac{1}{4}$ days
Jupiter			
Pluto			

> You do not need to scan for information about the Earth as it is already given. This entry shows you how to record the information for the other planets

Test yourself!

Use the information from page 24 to fill in this table of facts about planets Mercury and Pluto.

The section on Earth has been completed for you.

Remember

Information is not always in one place. Keep scanning and reading until you find all the information you need.

Inferring – looking for clues

Answers are not always obvious. They cannot always be found by simply scanning and picking out the relevant fact. Sometimes the information you want is not in the actual words on the page, but you can **infer** it (find clues about it) from the information given. This is why it is important to think about the information you are given as you are reading.

In a situation like this, think about what you are being asked. Read the relevant part of the text again, thinking about the information you **are** given. Then decide what this would lead you to think about the subject.

Here is a question that asks you to find some information.

> Read this information about elephants.
> **Decide:** Are elephants a danger to man?

There are two types of elephant, the African elephant and the smaller Indian elephant. Elephants are the largest and most powerful land mammals alive today. Despite their size they can charge if necessary, although they cannot maintain speed for very long. They are vegetarians, eating mainly grass, leaves and roots, which they gather with their trunks. They have large tusks, which are actually overgrown front teeth. Unfortunately, in the past elephants have been hunted to near extinction for the ivory of their tusks...

Nowhere in the passage does it say whether elephants can kill or hurt people. However, there are a lot of clues in the passage that might help you to answer this question:

> Elephants are the largest and most powerful land mammals...
> ... they can charge...
> They have large tusks...

However, on the other hand it also says:

> They are vegetarians...
> ... they have been hunted...

From these clues, you might suggest that a charging elephant with large tusks would be a danger to anyone in its path. However, elephants have little reason to charge at people, unless in self-defence. The text says that elephants have been hunted to near extinction. Therefore you might also suggest that elephants have more reason to be scared of people.

Test yourself!

In parts of Asia, elephants have traditionally been trained to work in timber mills.

Use the information from the passage (above left) to explain why trained elephants are useful in timber mills.

Remember

Sometimes you have to think about what you are told and come to a conclusion of your own.

The non-fiction author's purpose

Writers of **non-fiction** texts have a range of reasons for writing. Their purpose might be to **explain**, **instruct**, **persuade**, **discuss**, **inform**, **describe** or **recount**. Often the writer makes his or her purpose clear, but sometimes you need to look for clues in the text that shows the purpose.

The title or the layout of the text may give you a clue. But the most important thing is to think as you read about **what the writer is trying to achieve.** Remember that some texts will have more than one purpose. As you read the examples of different text types, below, see if you can think of any examples of your own.

Instructions

Purpose: to tell the reader how to achieve something

Examples: How to make flapjacks, How to program your video

> You will find more information about the different types of non-fiction writing on pages 58 to 63.

Explanation

Purpose: to explain a process, for example how something works, how or why something happens

Examples: The life cycle of the butterfly, How shadows are formed

Persuasive writing

Purpose: to put a point of view and to convince the reader to agree with it

Examples: Save the whale, Join the healthy eating club

Discussion

Purpose: to present different points of view on an issue

Examples: The pros and cons of television, Should mobile phones be allowed in schools?

Test yourself!

Match each of these sentences to the type of non-fiction text that it comes from:

1 Brachiosaurus, a plant-eater, was the largest land animal ever known...
2 Next add the oats and mix well.
3 As soon as we clambered off the coach it began to rain...

Report

Purpose: to describe and give information about a given subject

Examples: Discovering dinosaurs, The planets in our Solar System

Recount

Purpose: to retell events that happened

Examples: Our visit to the zoo, Columbus's journey to America

Remember

Non-fiction texts are written for different purposes.

How non-fiction texts are presented

Non-fiction texts are organised and presented differently from fiction texts. You will notice that features such as **text boxes**, **bold print**, **bullet points**, **tables of information** and **diagrams** are often used in non-fiction texts. These features are used to help **present information clearly**. They make it easier for you, the reader, to **find the information you need**.

Look out for these features. Think about **why** the writer has chosen to use them and **how they will help you** to read the text effectively.

Here is an example of an article about bird watching. Look at how the information has been presented.

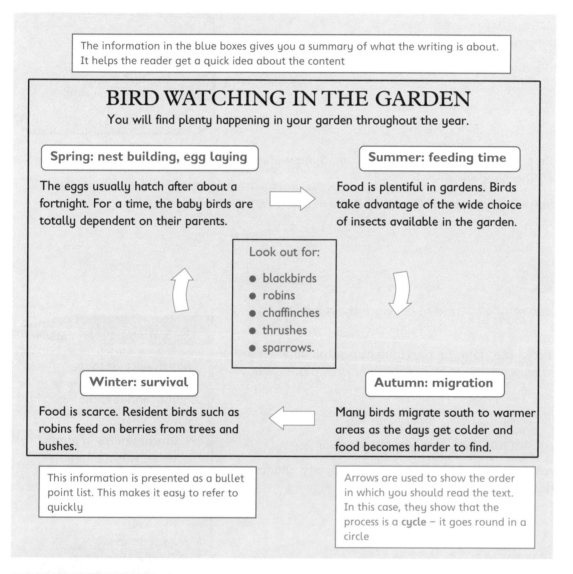

The information in the blue boxes gives you a summary of what the writing is about. It helps the reader get a quick idea about the content

BIRD WATCHING IN THE GARDEN
You will find plenty happening in your garden throughout the year.

Spring: nest building, egg laying

The eggs usually hatch after about a fortnight. For a time, the baby birds are totally dependent on their parents.

Summer: feeding time

Food is plentiful in gardens. Birds take advantage of the wide choice of insects available in the garden.

Look out for:

- blackbirds
- robins
- chaffinches
- thrushes
- sparrows.

Winter: survival

Food is scarce. Resident birds such as robins feed on berries from trees and bushes.

Autumn: migration

Many birds migrate south to warmer areas as the days get colder and food becomes harder to find.

This information is presented as a bullet point list. This makes it easy to refer to quickly

Arrows are used to show the order in which you should read the text. In this case, they show that the process is a **cycle** – it goes round in a circle

Test yourself!

In a set of instructions called **How to make a kite**, why do you think the following features are used?

1 The items needed are presented as a **bullet point list**
2 **Numbers** are placed by each of the points
3 **Diagrams** are used next to some of the instructions

Remember

Look at **how** the information is presented. Think about **why** it is presented in this way and how it helps you.

Illustrations in non-fiction

Illustrations are used differently in non-fiction and fiction texts. In non-fiction, the illustrations are usually used to **give information** or to help **explain** points made in the text. For this reason the illustrations will usually have **captions** and sometimes **labels** to point out the most important features. It is important that you read the captions to understand the point of the illustration.

You should also look out for illustrations that are used to **create impact** rather than to give information. These are found particularly in **persuasive texts**.

What types of illustration are found in a non-fiction text?

Photographs

Photographs help the text to look realistic. They can also be used for impact.

Drawings

Illustrations can be specially drawn to illustrate something in the text.

Diagrams

Diagrams give exact information. Labels may point out particular parts. Diagrams are used a lot in explanations and instructions to help the reader follow the text.

Cartoon-style illustrations

Cartoons are often used to capture the reader's attention or to make a point in a humorous way.

Why are illustrations used?

To give an example

Some illustrations help to explain the text by giving an example. An article on African wildlife might describe how some animals use camouflage for protection. A photograph or drawing is then included showing a particular animal camouflaged against the landscape.

> **Test yourself!**
>
> A leaflet asking for donations to support a shelter for homeless pets includes a large close-up photograph of a puppy.
>
> Why did the author choose to include this photograph?

To make things clear

Sometimes it is easier to **show** than to describe. For example, in the instructions on the right, a diagram is used to show exactly where to make the hole.

5. Make a hole near the side of the mask. (See diagram.)

To make an impact

Illustrations may be used for their impact and what they suggest to the reader. Persuasive texts such as adverts often use illustrations in this way. Attractive photographs are used to appeal to the reader.

> **Remember**
>
> You need to 'read' the illustrations as well as the text.

The non-fiction author's point of view

It is easy to forget that non-fiction writing has an author. You might think that everything you read in a non-fiction book is pure fact. But this is not always the case. Sometimes, writers are not just trying to **inform** their readers, but also to **persuade** them to agree with their point of view.

Sometimes, writers give **balanced factual information**. Sometimes they hold a particular opinion and this **influences the information** they give or **how they present** the information. It is important to look out for signs of an author's viewpoint when you are reading. Think about what you learn of the author's viewpoint as you read the examples below.

Fact and opinion

This writer provides information about a ruined building:

> The ruins of Mately Hall stand on the banks of the river. Originally built in the 1570s, during the reign of Elizabeth I, it was the home of the Mately family for 350 years. After a fire in 1922, the family could not afford to restore the building and it has been left as a ruin ever since. It is a crime that such a magnificent building should be left unprotected…

> This sentence shows the writer's point of view. The rest of the information is **fact**, but this is an **opinion**. The writer wants us to agree with this opinion

A biased point of view

Here is another example. This one is taken from a newspaper report on a football match:

> … Rovers were <u>unlucky</u> to lose their lead just before half time. Robinson was <u>clearly</u> offside as he shot past the goalkeeper, but the linesman <u>failed to notice</u>. The Rovers players had every right to protest.

> The words underlined suggest that the reporter is biased towards Rovers. It is a **fact** that Robinson scored. It is an opinion that it was a lucky goal

'Biased' means giving an opinion without showing the views of others.

Test yourself!

Read this paragraph. Find the phrase that gives the opinion of the writer rather than being a definite fact:

> The author Tamsin Black wrote her first novel in 1992. Since then she has written 20 books and has become the best current writer of realistic stories. Her new novel is to be published soon.

Remember

Look out for signs of a writer's **point of view**. Know what is **fact** and what is **opinion**.

Sources and opinions

Different authors have different views and opinions. It can be useful to read and compare a range of different authors' writing about the same subject. Notice the differences in the information included, how the information is presented and the opinions of the author.

Some writers choose to present the reader with a range of different points of view, or information from a number of different sources. In this case they might include quotations from people who have different viewpoints on the subject.

Here are some examples of how authors use quotations.

Someone who was there

This example is taken from a newspaper report on a fire in a warehouse. The quotation is from someone who was actually present at the event:

Mrs Brown described the scene as: 'Terrifying. The smoke was so thick everything went dark. It was just like the middle of the night.'

This sort of quotation gives a vivid first hand description of what it was like to be there

Someone who is an expert

Authors also use quotations from people who are experts in a particular subject. For example in an article on Historic Buildings the writer includes this quotation:

Professor Ballinger of the Buildings Protection League says: 'This building is very important in helping us to understand the history of the local area.'

Quotations from experts are particularly useful for supporting opinions or points of view because they come from someone who knows the subject well

Someone with a different point of view

An author might use quotations to help present two different views on a subject. For example, the author of the article on Historic Buildings might balance out the quotation above with this one:

Why worry about the history of the area? The future is much more important!

Test yourself!

Here is another quotation from the newspaper report on the fire.

Fire-Fighter Daljit Singh said: 'The warehouse contained a lot of highly flammable material, which gave off toxic fumes and thick black smoke. Conditions were very difficult for the fire-fighters.'

Why has the reporter included this quotation in the report?

Remember

Quotations from **different sources** can offer **different points of view**.

The non-fiction author's methods

Non-fiction writers have to **capture the interest of their readers** and **make them think** about the information being presented. In addition, writers might also want to give a point of view and get their readers to agree with them.

Writers of non-fiction use many of the same techniques as writers of stories. Look out for the ways in which a writer captures your interest or makes you think about what they say. Think about the **words chosen** and **how things are presented**, as well as **the information itself**.

The following techniques or methods are used by non-fiction authors. Can you think of any others?

Descriptive language and imagery

The trees in a rainforest form a vast rooftop garden.

In the second half of the match, Simmons played with about as much grace as an injured rhinoceros.

Comparisons like these should **create a picture in your head** that suggests a particular feature of what is being described, e.g. the colourful richness of the rainforest, or the clumsy quality of the footballer's play.

Speaking directly to the reader

Are you BMX crazy?

How would you like to live in the middle of a desert?

Should pupils be allowed to take their mobile phones into the classroom? What do you think?

Questions like these might be used to **capture your interest** or to **make you think** about the information just given.

Exclamations

Amazing offer!   Killer crocodiles!

Exclamations are used for **impact**. They **catch your attention** and make you read that part of the text.

Remember

Think about **how** writers present information as well as what they say.

Test yourself!

Read this information from a book called *Discovering Dinosaurs*:

Tyrannosaurus Rex
A meat-eater, the Tyrannosaurus Rex (also known as T. Rex) could open its mouth wide enough to eat 70kg of meat in just one bite. Always on the look out for food, T. Rex was like a mouth on legs!

Why does the writer describe T. Rex as being like 'a mouth on legs'?

Responding to non-fiction

It is important to be able to make **judgements** and offer **opinions** on non-fiction writing. For example, you might compare two sources on the same subject, saying which you preferred or which was most suitable for a particular task.

As with your personal response to stories, it is important that you **back up your opinions** by explaining or giving examples from the text. Ask yourself **why** you found a text useful, interesting or easy to read. Think about **why** you found another text less interesting and not so useful. Think about different aspects of the texts.

You can read about responding to fiction on page 15 and responding to poems on page 17.

An example of a personal response

This is a personal response to two different texts on endangered animals.

> The first text gives you factual information. The author uses text boxes and bullet points to present the information. This makes it easy to pick out key facts. The second text gives the writer's point of view on what should be done to save these animals. I preferred this text as it made me think more, especially when the writer says: 'Imagine a world with no wild animals.'

Notice that the response refers to **both** texts, commenting on the different purposes and features of each.

> A personal opinion is supported by a reason and an example or quotation from the text

Giving your personal response – some hints

Remember to comment on different features of the text. Here are some things to think about:

- **How the text is presented**
  Was it easy to find the information you needed? Why? What features helped you?

- **The author's purpose**
  What is the author's purpose? Is he or she successful? Why/Why not?

- **Who the text is aimed at**
  Is it aimed at adults and too complicated? Or aimed at young children and too simple? What makes you say that?

- **The author's point of view**
  Did the writer have a particular angle? Was there a hidden message? What makes you say that?

- **Techniques used**
  How did the author capture your interest and keep you interested? What did you like or dislike about how the author presented the information?

Test yourself!

Think of a non-fiction text you have used recently in another subject.

Which of these words would you use to describe the text?

**Interesting   Confusing
Easy to use   Useful**

Explain your choice by referring to the text.

Remember

Always **back up your comments** by giving **reasons** and using **examples** from the text.

Writing stories – starting points

You always need an **idea** to start a story off. Thinking of an idea can often be the hardest part of writing a story. Of course, you may find that you are given a starting point for your story and then have to develop a story around it.

The **starting point** might be a **story title**, an **opening sentence** to use at the start of your story, or just an **idea** of what the story might be about. You should **use these ideas** in your story and **add some ideas of your own**. Read the starting point carefully and look for clues about the sort of story you are being asked to write.

Here is an example of a starting point for a story.

Starting with a character

> The main character in the story is quiet and shy. Someone who is never noticed in the crowd.
>
> Write the story of what happens one day when this character becomes the centre of attention.
>
> Think about what the main character is like.
> What happens on this one particular day?
> How do other characters react to the events?

Here, you are given some important details about the main character – but not everything. Is the character a boy or a girl? A child or an adult? Or even an animal!

What you do know is that the main character is usually quiet and shy, but something unusual happens in the story to get him or her noticed. You must base your story on this information.

Starting with the story opening

> A visit to Mrs Donaldson's was not something we looked forward to. But this particular day it turned out to be the start of an amazing adventure.

This time, you are given the start of the story. This gives you plenty of clues about the sort of story you are going to write. It is going to be an adventure story and will need to be written in the first person. The story starts at Mrs Donaldson's house, but may change setting as the adventure develops.

Test yourself!

Read this idea for a story. Underline the important information that you will need to include in your story:

> I thought this new computer game was great, until suddenly something strange happened. This was the start of an amazing adventure...

Remember

Read the **starting point** carefully. Look for the **main ideas** that you will need to use in your story.

Developing ideas

Once you have identified the **key ideas** in the starting point for the story, you can begin to **develop your story**. There are some important things to **decide** right at the start and then **stick to** when you are actually writing your story, for example:

- What sort of story (or genre) is it going to be?
- Who is going to tell the story?

Having read the story task, you might find that the answers to these questions have already been decided for you. In that case, you must stick to the ideas you have been given.

What sort of story is it?

The story might be:

- a **realistic** story set in school or at home
- a **fantasy** story set in some amazing world
- an **adventure** story with exciting events
- a **mystery** with a problem to solve
- a **traditional** style story.

The first story on page 34 (about the quiet, shy character) would work well as a **realistic** story set at school or home. The second story (about the visit to Mrs Donaldson's) might be realistic, but it should also have elements of **adventure** and perhaps even **fantasy**.

Who is going to tell the story?

The story can be told in the **third person**, as if you are watching the events and describing what happened to the characters. For example:

> Sam dawdled down the street with his head down, his eyes fixed on the pavement before him.

If you prefer, you can tell the story in the **first person**, as if you are one of the characters in the story.

> A visit to Mrs Donaldson's was not something we usually enjoyed.

> This story opening is written in the first person. That means you must continue to write your story in this way. You can't change. Otherwise it will sound confusing

Test yourself!

I thought this new computer game was great, until suddenly something strange happened. This was the start of an amazing adventure…

What **sort** of story are you being asked to write?

Who is going to **tell** the story?

Remember

Decide what **sort** of story you are going to write and then **stick to it**.

Don't change half way through!

Planning a story

When authors write a **novel**, they have the chance to develop ideas slowly, over time. When you are writing a **short story** in a limited amount of time, you have to keep the story tight and the events moving. For this reason, it is important to **plan** your story before you start writing.

Before you start writing, you should be clear about the **main characters**, the **setting of the story**, what happens at the **start of the story**, the **sequence of events** that follow and how the story is going to end.

Here is an example of how you might plan your story.

Story plan

The characters in the story
- Taz – a boy – quiet and shy
- Vic – his friend – outgoing

> In a short story, only have two or three characters

The setting: where and when
Classroom – busy
School football pitch – excited, cheering crowds

> You only need to make short notes on your plan. Just write down brief ideas or words and phrases to use in your writing

How the story begins

> (Read more about plotting the main events on page 37)

The main events in the story

How the story ends

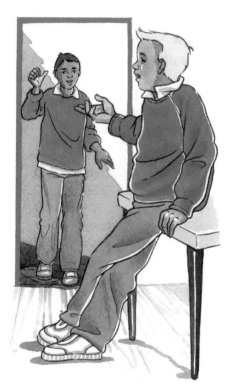

Test yourself!

Start to write a plan for the computer game story from the **Test yourself!** box on page 35.

Decide on the characters and the setting/s.
Make notes like those shown above.

Then read **Plotting events** (page 37).

Remember

Always **plan** your story before you start writing.

Plotting events

Plotting out the main events in the story is very important. It is useful to have a **trigger event** very early on in your story. A trigger event is something that **starts the story off**. The rest of the events will then follow on from this event until you reach a satisfying end to your story.

Try thinking about the plot as **a chain of events**, with all the events linked together, leading to the end of the story. Each **event** is **one link** in the chain. If an important event is missing, then the chain is broken.

Chain of events

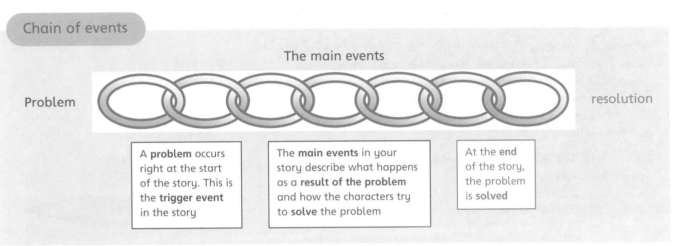

The main events

Problem   resolution

A **problem** occurs right at the start of the story. This is the **trigger event** in the story

The **main events** in your story describe what happens as a **result of the problem** and how the characters try to **solve** the problem

At the **end** of the story, the problem is **solved**

Trigger events

Possible trigger events that might start a story off include:

- the main character finds, or is given, something with magic powers
- the main character sees something that causes him or her to be amazed, worried, concerned...
- something unusual and unexpected happens.

An example of a story plan

Here is an example of what a chain of events might look like on a story plan:

The main events in the story

- main character sees a shop being broken into (the **trigger event**)
- follows the thieves to their hide out – recognises them
- nearly caught, but escapes
- reports the events to the police
- the thieves are captured (**how the story ends**).

Test yourself!

Go back to your plan for the computer game story (see **Test yourself!** pages 35 and 36).

Complete your plan by plotting **how the story begins**, the **main events** and **how the story ends**.

Remember

Think of the **plot** as **links in a chain** – linking the **trigger event** to the **end** of the story.

Using paragraphs in fiction

As you write your story, use paragraphs to make the chain of events clear to the reader. Start a new paragraph for each new event that happens, or for each link in the chain. Following your story plan will help you know when to start a new paragraph.

It is also a good idea to start a new paragraph each time you introduce a change of time or place. A **connective** can be used at the start of a paragraph, to show the reader how the story has moved on.

Starting a new paragraph

<u>In the afternoon</u>, everyone became more and more excited as the hour of the match approached. Most of 6B found it hard to concentrate on their history project, particularly when they could hear the preparations going on outside. Taz, on the other hand, was quite happy to bury his head in a book and escape into the past for a while.

After school, Taz followed the crowd to the football pitch at the side of the school…

> A new paragraph is needed here because the story has moved on in time. The phrase **After school** is used to link the two paragraphs

Using connectives to start a new paragraph

Change of time

You can use connectives (connecting words and phrases) at the start of paragraphs to tell your reader about movements in time. For example:

After…   After a while…   Suddenly…   The next day…
Later…   Eventually…

Change of place

The following phrases are useful for keeping your reader informed of changes in setting:

Back at school…   On the other side of the river…
In the loft…   Far away, on the red planet…

Test yourself!

Read this extract from a story. Decide where the writer should have started a new paragraph, and explain why.

As we drank our tea, Mrs Donaldson rambled on, telling us her strange stories. She was desperate to show us some old photographs and insisted we go into the loft to find them. Up in the loft it was dark and dusty. The dust made me sneeze and the loft was so crowded it was difficult to find anything.

Remember

Follow your plan – start a new paragraph for each new event, or each change in time or place.

Interesting openings

Giving your story an **interesting opening** is very important. You need to **capture the interest of your readers** and make them want to read on. Starting your story with the words 'One day, …' is not going to do this.

There are many better ways of starting a story. For example you might try using **description**, **action** or **dialogue**. Whatever you choose, make sure your story opening **sets a mood** or **introduces something important** about the characters, the setting, or the subject of the story.

Examples of some different starting points are given below.

Starting with description

This could be description of the **main character,** or description of the **setting**. Try to make the description of a character suggest something **interesting** about them:

> Mrs Donaldson opened her front door. Her inquisitive eyes peered at us through thick lenses.

Or use description of a setting to create an immediate picture or develop an atmosphere:

> Mrs Donaldson's house was as old and untidy as she was.

Starting with action

Starting with a **dramatic event** will capture the interest of readers, because they will want to find out **what is happening and why**:

> Thud! A box of books fell from the top of the wardrobe onto the dusty floor.

Starting with dialogue

Dialogue can be used to introduce characters or events at the start of a story. It can intrigue the readers and make them want to find out more…

> 'Do we have to go?' I pleaded. 'Mrs Donaldson is such a bore.' 'Really, Nick – you should be more sympathetic! She's a poor old lady who relies on us for a bit of company,' replied my sister, in her most superior voice.

You can read more about **using dialogue** on pages 44 and 45.

Remember

You can start your story with **description**, **action** or **dialogue**.

Test yourself!

Write **three** different opening sentences for the computer game story (see **Test yourself!** on pages 35, 36 and 37). Write one sentence using **description**, one using **action** and one using **dialogue**.

Developing characters

Interesting characters help to make **interesting stories**. The main characters in your story need to be more than just names. When you are planning your story, you should decide **what they look like** and, more importantly, **what sort of people** they are.

Keep these facts in your mind as you write your story. Think about how a character would **behave**, **speak** or **feel** at different points. Work into your story all these details about the character.

The examples below show different ways in which a character might be developed in a story. Notice that it only needs one sentence to feed in each important detail.

Planning a character

First, decide who the character is and what his or her main qualities are. Then make some notes on your plan. For example:

Taz – a boy – quiet and shy

Describing appearance

In your story, describe something about the character's appearance. Don't try to describe everything, but choose key features that will give your reader a picture of the character. Try doing this in one interesting sentence, rather than a long description. For example:

Taz had a thin face and dark thoughtful eyes.

Adding details

Feed in some details about what sort of person the character is. For example, you might suggest that Taz is shy through the way he behaves:

Taz tried to hide at the back of the crowd of jostling bodies, hoping to remain hidden from view.

Showing feelings

Show the feelings of your main character and his or her reaction to events. For example, to show that Taz is nervous at a certain point in the story you might write:

Taz stood on the touchline. Not just his knees were shaking – his whole body trembled.

Using contrasting characters

It can sometimes be useful to have contrasting characters in your story. Then you can show the differences between them. For example, Taz might have a friend who is confident and outgoing:

There was Vic, at the centre of things as always.

Test yourself!

Here is an idea for a character in a story:

Jess – a girl – slightly bossy, an older sister

Write one sentence to describe something important about Jess's appearance. Write another sentence showing that she is slightly bossy.

Remember

Feed in **details** that **show** what **sort of person** your main character is.

Developing settings

You need to make it clear to the reader **when** and **where** the events in your story take place. You may have a clear picture of this in your head, but you need to create a picture for the reader as well.

As with describing characters, the best way to describe settings is to include **small details** about important sights and sounds, rather than write lengthy descriptions. You can also use description of a setting to help create a **mood** or **feeling** about the place or the events about to happen.

Planning settings

Make a note on your story plan of the setting or settings to be featured in your story. Include some short, key phrases to describe them. For example:

Classroom – busy, messy, slightly chaotic
Magician's cave – amazing – also messy, <u>very</u> chaotic

Including details

In your story you need to develop these ideas by including details that describe the setting. Think about the main sights and noises that create a picture of the place:

The classroom was flooded with excited chatter and discarded scraps of paper.

Describing settings

Describing what a place looks like is particularly important with a fantasy setting. You have a picture in your head, but you need to describe this for your reader. This is one occasion where a longer, more detailed description is needed:

The shelves on the walls were stacked with glass containers, each holding a different coloured liquid. Some liquids were bubbling, some were fizzing. Some jars were clear, some were murky...

You can also use details about a setting to help create a mood in your story. Compare these two examples:

It was late and the sky was growing dark. Strange noises came from amongst the trees.

Laughter echoed in the lazy afternoon sunshine.

Notice that details about weather, time, light and noise are particularly useful for creating mood.

Test yourself!

Here is an idea for a setting of a story:

Supermarket – very busy.

Decide on some details that you might feed into the story to show that it is set in a busy supermarket.

Remember

Describe details about the settings in your story. Use the setting to help create mood.

Effective endings

It is important to give your story a **good ending**, otherwise your reader will be disappointed! At the end of the story, all **problems** and **mysteries** that you have introduced through the main events must be **solved**. That does not mean the ending has to be obvious. You can still give your story a **surprise ending**, something that solves the problem in an unexpected way.

It is particularly important to **make your final sentence memorable** – for example, by giving a comment on the events, or on the characters' feelings.

Let's suppose that this is what happens at the end of the story about the children who visit Mrs Donaldson:

> The two children have reached a strange world through the door of old Mrs Donaldson's attic. They were captured by a wizard, but then managed to escape. They are now racing back to find the door to the attic, chased by the wizard's dragon.

Here is one possible ending for the story:

> The dragon's fiery breath was scorching my neck. We could see the door amongst the trees, but it was beginning to close. This was our only chance of escape! We both dived forward, and somehow managed to scramble through the door just in time. The door closed and we lay in a breathless heap on the dusty attic floor. Never again would I laugh at Mrs Donaldson's stories of wizards and dragons.

> The story ends with a **comment** on how the events change the character's attitudes

Here is another ending for the same story. This time there is a surprise:

> The dragon's fiery breath was scorching my neck. There was no escape. Then, suddenly, in front of us appeared a figure. It was Mrs Donaldson! Mrs Donaldson, dressed in a purple cloak, arms raised above her head. With a crackle, sparks flew from her fingers and the dragon immediately shrank to the size of a mouse. 'Such a nuisance these dragons, if you don't know how to deal with them. Come on you two – it must be time for you to go home...'

In this version, it is a surprise when Mrs Donaldson comes to rescue the children.

Test yourself!

Imagine that you are writing the ending of the computer game story (see **Test yourself!** pages 34 to 37 and page 39). The adventure is over and the main characters are safe at home. Write a last line for the story that is better than this one:

> We went downstairs to have our tea.

Remember

Think of an **interesting way** of **ending** your story. The **last line** is **particularly important**.

Using description

Description is a powerful tool for writing good stories. Description can help you to create pictures for your reader of characters, settings and events. It can also help to create a mood or atmosphere.

Describing things well is all about **choosing the best words**, rather than using the first word that comes into your head. Try to think of a word that describes exactly what you want to say. Avoid the words and expressions that we use every day.

Here are some examples of how choosing the right word can make your writing more effective.

> Adjectives and adverbs can help to make your writing interesting. Read about them on pages 65 and 66.

Improving on first thoughts

This is the sort of sentence that might come straight into your head:

> He walked through the wood.

Here are some examples of how the sentence might be improved by choosing words more carefully:

> Terrified, he scrambled his way through the grasping branches of the trees.

> He sauntered through the welcome shade of the woods.

The careful choice of words not only changes the picture created – it also changes the mood. While the first sentence creates a feeling of fear, the second sounds relaxed and pleasant.

Choosing interesting words

Imagine that you are about to bring a car into your story. There are hundreds of words you could use to describe it. You have to choose the words that most accurately describe the car you mean. Avoid common choices, and choose interesting, colourful words:

Rather than: a big shiny car ✗
Make it: a magnificent gleaming vehicle ✓

Rather than: a tatty old car ✗
Make it: an antiquated ramshackle machine ✓

> **Remember**
>
> **Choose words carefully** to describe **settings, characters** and **events** and to **create moods.**

Test yourself!

Imagine that you wanted to introduce a house into your story. Choose more interesting and accurate words to improve these descriptions:

A big new house

A small old house

Using dialogue

Dialogue (**direct speech**) is another important element in story writing. However, you should make sure that the dialogue you write is **useful to the story**, not just a pointless conversation.

Dialogue between characters can be used to **show what is happening** in the story, or to **give information about characters**. A conversation between two characters is particularly useful for showing the **relationship between them**.

You can use both **direct** and **reported** speech in a story. **Direct** speech is useful if you want to show the reader something about the characters. **Reported** speech is useful if you want to summarise quickly what was said.

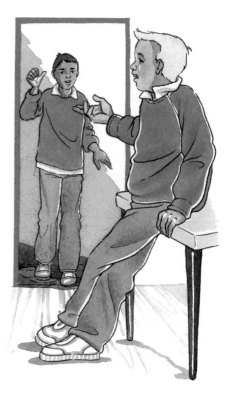

Direct speech

In this first example, the dialogue has little point because it adds nothing to the story:

> 'Hello,' said Vic.
> 'Hello, said Taz.
> 'It's a nice day,' said Vic.
> 'Yes it is,' said Taz.

This dialogue is pointless because it tells us nothing about the characters or about the events in the story. Now look at this second example:

> 'Hi there,' shouted Vic, from amongst a crowd of people.
> 'Oh, hello Vic,' said Taz shyly.
> 'Great day for a football match, don't you think?'
> 'I suppose it is. I had forgotten it was the match tonight,' admitted Taz.

Here we learn something about what is happening in the story (there is to be a football match) and something about the characters (Taz is shy and less interested in the match than Vic; Taz and Vic are friends).

Reported speech

With reported speech, you do not write down every word said, instead you summarise the main point. For example:

> Taz admitted that he had forgotten about the match.

Test yourself!

Write a short exchange of dialogue between two characters. One of them has just found an old key and is eager to find out what it belongs to. Use the dialogue to present this situation to the reader.

Remember

Use **dialogue** in your story to show **what is happening** or to show **what characters are like**.

Using dialogue

Writing dialogue

When you are writing dialogue it is important to set it out properly so that it is easy for the reader to follow. In direct speech you should:

- use **speech marks** – to show which words are actually said
- start a **new line** when a **different person** starts to speak – to show clearly who says what
- write short clauses that **say who is speaking** – try not to keep using the word 'said': other choices provide variety and can show the feelings of the character speaking.

Here is an example of dialogue from a story. Notice how a **new line** is started each time a new person starts to speak.

Speech marks to show the words actually spoken	Different words used instead of said

'Where have you been?' demanded Amanda. 'I said six o'clock.'
'Sorry, I just couldn't get away,' sighed Jo.
'Well it's too late now isn't it? They've already gone,' complained Amanda.
'Sorry,' repeated Jo sadly.
'Hm, well I suppose it can't be helped. Come on let's see if we can catch them up.'

Comma between the spoken and non-spoken words	No need to say who is speaking here. We can tell from the flow of the conversation

Saying who is speaking and how

In the example above, some different words are used instead of 'said'. Here are some more alternatives – there are hundreds to choose from.

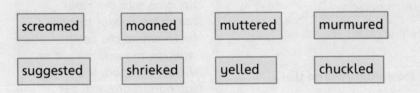

An adverb can be used in dialogue to show **how** a character says something. You can add this 'how' word to the verb – e.g., 'he said coldly'. Here are some examples of useful adverbs.

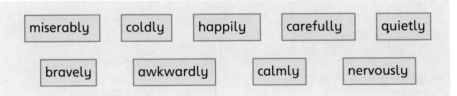

Test yourself!

Set out this dialogue properly:

Kris heard someone call his name. Chaz! Chaz! Is that you? Where are you? Kris shouted. I'm over here, behind the fireplace. There's some sort of secret tunnel said the voice. How did you get in there? asked Kris feeling around the fireplace for a lever or a handle.

Remember

Set out dialogue properly so that it is always clear to the reader **which character is speaking.**

Style in fiction

Writing a good story is not just about ideas, but also about **how** you tell the story. As you write, try thinking about the readers and how you can keep them interested in the story you are telling. To find out how interesting your story is, it is a good idea to read it aloud and see how it sounds.

You might try **speaking directly to the reader**, or using **questions** that make the reader think about the results of an action. You can also try **commenting** on the events or on the feelings of the characters. These techniques will work with stories told in the first person and those told in the third person.

Speaking directly to your reader

Here are some examples of how you can speak directly to your reader and **comment on events**.

A first person story

This example is from a story told in the first person:

> Well, you can imagine what a disaster it was. Dad had absolutely **no idea** about cooking on a camp fire. I tell you, there was no way I was eating one of those sausages!

The writing sounds informal because it is written in the first person, from the point of view of the child. The comments on the events make it seem as though the narrator is speaking directly to the reader.

A third person story

This example is from a story told in the third person:

> Jamie knew now there was no escape. Despite all his efforts, he was still trapped within the castle.

Here, the writer's comments make clear the seriousness of the situation.

Using questions

Another technique you can try is to use questions to make the reader think about what will happen next.

Some examples of questions that draw the reader in

> But what if he was wrong? What if that was **not** the way out? What if there was **no** way out? Was it too late?

> Surely it would not matter if she took just one bite? What could happen?

Test yourself!

Imagine that the main character in your story is faced with a choice – whether to press the red or the blue button. Making the right choice will get them back home safely.

Write this part of the story using questions and comments to build up the tension and excitement.

Remember

Speak directly to your reader, using **questions** and **comments** to draw the reader in to your story.

Style in fiction

No one wants to read a dull story, so it is important to **build up the excitement** in your story. Always make sure there is at least one really exciting part in your story. It is best if this comes **towards the end**, so that you can build up to the most thrilling moment. This keeps your readers interested.

When making something sound exciting, it is a good idea to keep the readers **in suspense**. Rather than tell the readers straightaway, **make them wait**. Use **description** to draw your readers in – and then **surprise** them...

Building up suspense – some hints

Here are some methods you could use to build up suspense and excitement:

- **describe each sound** – rather than saying what it is
- **create doubt**
- **use questions** that draw the reader in
- **show how the main character is feeling**
- sometimes use a **very short sentence for effect**
- **use exclamations for a sudden impact**.

An example ... footsteps in the tunnel!

This exciting passage uses some of the above techniques to build suspense.

A one-word sentence for effect	Questions to draw the reader in

Footsteps. Where were they coming from? Jamie froze flat against the tunnel wall. There was silence now, apart from the dripping of water. All he could hear was his own unsteady breathing. Should he continue? He did not know who else was in the tunnel, or where the echoing sounds had come from.

Shows how the character is feeling	Creating doubts about who and where	Sounds

Test yourself!

Describe what happened when the character presses the red or blue button (see **Test yourself!** page 46).

Use some of the techniques described on this page to build up the excitement.

Remember

Use clever writing and **writer's techniques** to create suspense and excitement.

Writing a script

You might be asked to present your story as a script (or 'playscript'), rather than as a narrative. The important thing to remember is that scripts tell the story using dialogue and action, rather than narrative and description.

When you are writing a script, **imagine it being performed** – are you making everything clear for the actors and the audience? You must use **dialogue** and **stage directions** to show **settings**, to put across what the **characters** are like and to make sure the audience can follow **what is happening**.

Making the setting clear

The setting of the scene is usually introduced at the start of the scene. For example:

Scene 1
In a classroom

However, further details can be introduced through the dialogue between characters:

Rashid: This room is a mess! There's paper everywhere.

> Dialogue in a script is set out like this so that it is easy to follow.

Showing characters

Characters can be built up through their actions and dialogue and also through **what other characters say about them**. For example:

Katherine: Luke, why do you have to ask so many questions?
It's really annoying.

You can show the **feelings** of a character through stage directions and notes to the actor. For example:

Katherine: (*Anxiously*) Come on Luke, let's go.
Someone might see us.

The **actions** of the characters can also be shown through stage directions:

Enter Luke, carrying a box.
He puts it on the table.

> Don't include too many stage directions – most of the script should be dialogue.

Making events clear

Dialogue between characters should also be used to make clear what is happening:

Katherine: What are you doing?
Luke: Looking for clues.

Test yourself!

Katherine: (*Anxiously*)   Come on Luke, let's go.
Someone might see us.

Write Luke's reply. Remember to set it out like a script. Try to suggest something about Luke's character, or what he is doing.

Remember

A **script** or **playscript** tells the story through **dialogue** and **stage directions**.

Non-fiction writing – the task

When you are given a non-fiction writing task, the first step is to **read the task carefully**. Look for these three important pieces of information:

- the **form** of the writing (**what** you are being asked to write)
- the **purpose** of the writing (**why** you are writing it)
- the **audience** (**who** you are writing for).

This information will help you to make decisions when you begin planning and writing. So make sure you know exactly what is required at the start.

Here are some examples of writing tasks. The notes explain some of the main points that you need to think about.

Writing a letter

The form: a letter. Letters need to be set out in a particular way

Your class is running a campaign encouraging people to recycle waste paper. You have noticed how much paper is thrown away in schools every day. Write a letter to the Local Education Authority informing them about the matter and persuading them to collect the paper for recycling.

The purpose: to inform and persuade

The audience: this tells you it will need to be a formal letter

Writing a diary or journal entry

The word **personal** suggests that the audience is you

The form: a diary or journal

Write an entry for a personal diary or journal. In it recount the events of a particularly exciting day out.

The purpose: to recount

Other **forms** of writing to look out for include:

leaflets ● reports ● interviews ● newsletters

Other **purposes** of writing include:

to explain ● to instruct ● to describe
to discuss ● to inform

Test yourself!

Read this writing task. Identify the **form** and **purpose** of the writing and the **audience** you are writing for:

As part of the class recycling campaign, you are asked to write a leaflet that will be sent home to parents telling them about the project and the importance of recycling.

The leaflet should inform the parents about recycling and persuade them to join in at home.

Remember

Always **read the task carefully**.

Identify: the **form**, **purpose** and **audience**.

Introductions and conclusions

All non-fiction writing needs to be **organised**. It is always useful to start with an **introduction** – a sentence or paragraph that introduces the subject and the purpose of the writing.

Your writing should always end with a **conclusion**. This might be a summing up, restating the main point, or giving a final comment. A conclusion helps to bring the writing to a tidy end, rather than sounding as if you have just run out of ideas.

Introductions

Set out the pros and cons

Here is an **introduction** for a leaflet discussing the pros and cons of building a ring road:

> The subject

It has been suggested that a ring road should be built around the town of Midvale. This would ease the traffic congestion within the town centre. However, there are people opposed to such a development. This leaflet aims to summarise the main points on each side of the argument.

> The purpose

Fit purpose, form and audience

The length and style of the introduction should fit the purpose, form and audience of the writing. Here is an introductory sentence for a set of instructions to appear in a children's comic:

> The purpose: instructions for how to make something

Halloween is just a few days away, so why not follow these instructions and make yourself a seriously spooky Halloween mask.

> The subject: making a mask for Halloween

> Sounds fun – as the instructions are for children

Conclusions

Writing **conclusions** can be difficult. Here are three hints that may help you:

- Give an **overall comment** on the event or activity described, for example:

  > Despite all the problems, it was probably the best holiday we have ever had.

- Give a **summary** or **restate the main point** already made, for example:

  > There are valuable arguments both for and against building the new ring road. It is important that all points of view are considered when reaching a decision on this important local issue.

- **Relate the information to the reader**, for example:

  > Remember that you, like people all over the world, experience every day changes in weather patterns caused by global warming.

Test yourself!

Reread the **Test yourself!** writing task on page 49. Write a short **introductory paragraph** for the leaflet. Remember to introduce the **subject** and the **purpose** of the leaflet.

Then try writing a **conclusion** for the same leaflet. In your conclusion **restate your main point** and **link the information** to **the reader**.

Remember

Non-fiction writing needs an **introduction** and a **conclusion**.

Planning – organising your ideas

As you read on page 50, non-fiction writing must be **organised**. You cannot just write down the ideas in the order they come into your head. So it is important to plan your writing first.

Start by deciding the **points you want to cover** in your writing (remembering to think about the **purpose** of your writing and the **prompts** that were given in the task). Then try to put these ideas **into order**. There may be some points that link together. If so, make sure these points follow each other in your **plan**.

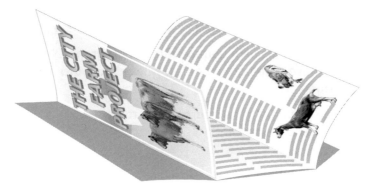

A non-fiction writing plan

This is the plan for an information leaflet to be given to people visiting a city farm. The city farm has only recently been set up and the leaflet aims to give information about the farm as well as help people enjoy their visit.

[Introduction: welcome visitors, explain purpose of leaflet]

Notice that short notes are all that is needed. These ideas will be developed when writing

[History of the farm – when and why it was set up]

[Details about the farm now – and the future]

It seems sensible to have the history of the farm, followed by the farm now

[Things to see and do during the visit]

[Reminders for visitors – caring for animals]

Each idea will be developed into a separate paragraph when you come to write the leaflet.

[Conclusion: thank the reader for their interest/ support]

Test yourself!

You have been asked to write a report on leisure activities available for young people in your local area. The report will be sent to local council members responsible for these facilities.

In your report you should outline the places and activities already available and explain what else is needed to improve the area. Make a writing plan. Read the task carefully for clues about what information you need to include. Decide what to include in the report, then put your ideas in order.

Remember

Always **organise** your ideas before you start writing.

Make a **plan**.

Using paragraphs in non-fiction

A **paragraph** is a **chunk of information**. Paragraphs are used to help **organise** your writing. A new paragraph is needed each time you **change subject** or start making a **new point**.

Having a plan will help you to write in paragraphs. Each **idea** you have noted on your plan will be **one paragraph** in your writing.

Here is an example of two paragraphs taken from a **letter of complaint**.

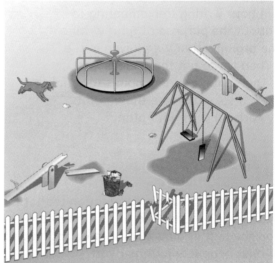

On arriving at the playground we found that many of the rides were broken and in a dangerous state. One of the see saws, for example, had been snapped off leaving a dangerous, rough edge that could have injured one of the children.

Moreover, the state of the playground itself was disgusting. There was litter everywhere…

A new paragraph is started here because the writer moves on to a new point. The first paragraph is about the broken rides; the second paragraph is about the litter in the playground

You can use **connectives** at the start of paragraphs to show the **links between ideas**.

Using connectives

In the example above, you will notice that the connective 'moreover' is used to link the points in the two paragraphs. Here are some other connectives that could be used to link paragraphs in your writing.

Connectives to use if you are making a **series of points**:

Furthermore ● In addition ● Also ● What is more
Additionally ● Finally

Connectives to use if you are about to offer a **different or contrasting view**:

However ● On the other hand ● In contrast ● Despite this

Test yourself!

Read again the extract from the letter of complaint, above. Complete the second paragraph, which describes the state of the playground.

Then write the first sentence for a third paragraph, praising a particularly helpful member of staff at the refreshments kiosk.

Remember

Start a **new paragraph** each time you start writing about a **new subject**.

Using paragraphs in non-fiction

Writing paragraphs

Always try to **organise** the **information** you give **within each paragraph**.

It is a good idea to start a paragraph with a **topic sentence** – this is a sentence that **introduces the main point of the paragraph**. Then in the rest of the paragraph you can **explain** that point further or **give examples** to back it up. Again, you can use a connective to help link ideas within a paragraph.

Here is an example of a paragraph that begins with a topic sentence and then explains the point further. It also uses connectives. The paragraph is taken from an e-mail that Fatima wrote to the company that made her mobile phone.

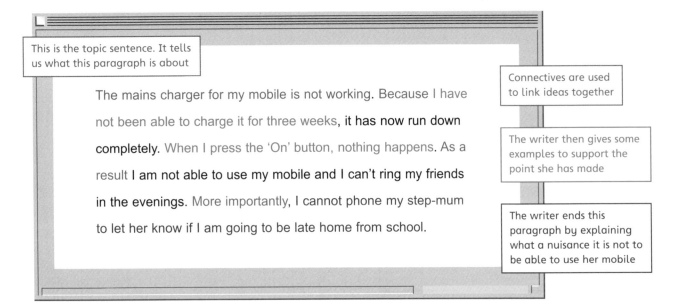

This is the topic sentence. It tells us what this paragraph is about

The mains charger for my mobile is not working. Because I have not been able to charge it for three weeks, **it has now run down completely.** When I press the 'On' button, nothing happens. **As a result** I am not able to use my mobile and I can't ring my friends in the evenings. More importantly, I cannot phone my step-mum to let her know if I am going to be late home from school.

Connectives are used to link ideas together

The writer then gives some examples to support the point she has made

The writer ends this paragraph by explaining what a nuisance it is not to be able to use her mobile

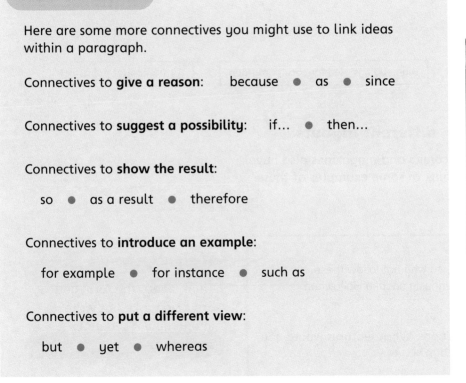

More connectives

Here are some more connectives you might use to link ideas within a paragraph.

Connectives to **give a reason**:   because ● as ● since

Connectives to **suggest a possibility**:   if... ● then...

Connectives to **show the result**:

so ● as a result ● therefore

Connectives to **introduce an example**:

for example ● for instance ● such as

Connectives to **put a different view**:

but ● yet ● whereas

Test yourself!

Read the plan on page 51 for the information leaflet about the city farm.

Write a **topic sentence** for **each of the four main paragraphs**. (You do **not** need to write sentences for the introduction and conclusion.)

Remember

Start each paragraph with a **topic sentence**.

Setting out your writing

Different **forms** of writing are **set out** in different ways. That is why it is important to know **what** you are being asked to write. For example, if you are asked to write a letter, you need to think about how letters are set out and presented. This is very different to how a leaflet, a report or a newspaper article would be set out.

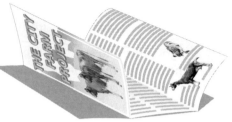

Whatever form of writing you are asked to write, think about examples you have seen. Decide how they are set out and use the same ideas in your own writing.

Setting out your writing for a leaflet

You need to remember the features below when you are writing a leaflet.

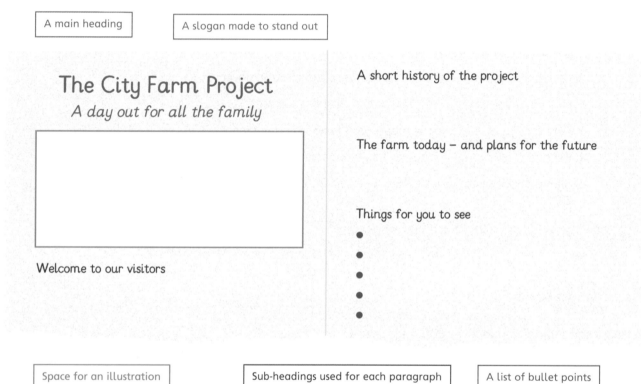

| A main heading |

| A slogan made to stand out |

The City Farm Project
A day out for all the family

Welcome to our visitors

A short history of the project

The farm today – and plans for the future

Things for you to see
-
-
-
-
-

| Space for an illustration |

| Sub-headings used for each paragraph |

| A list of bullet points |

Different forms of writing – different layouts

Newspapers, instructions, articles in comics and magazines also have their own special layout features. Think of some examples of these forms and how they are set out.

Test yourself!

Halloween is just a few days away, so why not follow these instructions and make yourself a seriously spooky Halloween mask.

You are asked to write these instructions. What features would you use to help you set out the information?

Remember

Think about the **form** you are being asked to write in and how it should be set out.

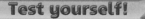

Setting out a letter

People write letters all the time. They can be written for many **different purposes**. You can write letters to explain, recount, to put a point of view, invite or complain… There are **formal** letters, written to people you have never met, and chatty, **informal letters** to friends and relations.

Letters have their own special layout. This is slightly different for a formal letter and an informal letter.

Here is an example of how a formal letter might be set out.

8, Green Lane
Sharpston
Lincolnshire
LL6 3PM

| Your address |

16/08/05

| Date |

Park Warden's Office
Council Towers
Clifton
Lincolnshire
LL6 5HY

| The address of the person you are writing to (this is only needed for formal letters) |

Dear Sir or Madam,

| Greeting (if you know the person's name, you would use it) |

I recently took my family for a day out at Clifton Park and am writing to complain about the terrible state of the children's playground.

| Explain why you are writing |

On arriving at the playground we found that many of the rides were broken and in a dangerous state. One of the seesaws, for example, had been snapped off leaving a dangerous, rough edge that could have injured one of the children.

Moreover, the state of the playground itself was disgusting. There was litter everywhere….

| The main part of the letter is written in paragraphs |

It is disgraceful that you let a children's playground get into this state. I hope something will be done to improve the situation or we will certainly not be visiting again.

Yours faithfully

Gillian Rogers

| Ending the letter (You would use a less formal phrase to end a letter to a friend) |

Mrs G Rogers

| Your signature or name |

Test yourself!

Imagine that you are writing a letter to a friend who has recently moved house.

1 How would you set out the letter?

2 What greeting might you use?

3 How would you end the letter?

Remember

Formal letters should be **set out differently** to friendly, informal letters.

The audience – formal or informal?

It is important to think about the people who will read what you are writing – your **audience**. This will help you to decide what style of writing you should use. Should your writing be formal or informal? **Informal** writing is usually used if you are writing to someone you actually **know**. **Formal** writing is used when you are writing for someone you **do not know**. However, you will probably use a more **informal** style if you are writing for a **young** audience or want to seem particularly **friendly**.

As you write, it is important to keep the reader in mind at all times so that you always use the right sort of language.

Informal writing

This is an extract from an informal letter, written to a friend:

> Exclamations and questions make the letter lively and personal

What an experience! I am never going on holiday with my family again – NEVER! First the car broke down. We'd only just made it onto the motorway, would you believe?

> Notice the use of shortened forms. You would not use these in formal writing

> This style is very chatty. It sounds like a normal conversation

A formal letter

> Typical formal phrases

I am writing on behalf of Class 6 at Redbridge School. We wish to enquire about the future plans for Redbridge Wood. It has come to our notice that this area is adjacent to a planned housing development and that the wood may be under threat.

> Very polite

> Formal or technical sounding words

Test yourself!

Read this rather formal introduction to an advertisement:

We wish to bring to your attention the new Kick-Start trainers.
Observe that they are particularly smart and comfortable.

Rewrite it in a **less formal style** that might appeal to children of your own age.

Remember

As you write, always **keep in mind the audience** you are writing for.

Formal writing

Writing in a **formal** style tends to be more difficult than **informal** writing.

Informal writing tends to be **chatty** and uses **everyday language**. It is often **personal** – you are writing about yourself.

Formal writing uses words and phrases that **we don't usually use** in normal conversation. It is deliberately **impersonal**.

Writing in a formal style – some hints

Here are five things to remember when you are writing in a formal style:

- **Imagine yourself as an adult**, particularly an important person, and think about how he or she would say or write things.

- Don't use everyday expressions. Instead, **use more formal ways of saying things**, for example:

  tell you about ✗ → inform you of ✓

  put up with ✗ → tolerate ✓

  ask ✗ → enquire ✓

- Use **precise technical words and phrases** related to the subject. For example, a report on recycling might use terms such as:

  > pollution ● atmosphere ● reusable ● sustain
  > conserve ● pulp ● recycling plant

- Use **more formal connectives**, rather than those we use in everyday speech:

  So ✗ → As a result… Consequently… Hence… ✓

  But ✗ → However,   Despite this ✓

- Use **passive** forms to make your writing impersonal:

Personal: *We use a microscope to see the cells.*

Impersonal: A microscope is used to see the cells.

Personal: *I think it is wrong to hunt foxes.*

Impersonal: Some people believe it is wrong to hunt foxes.

Test yourself!

This is supposed to be the opening of a formal discussion, but it does not sound very formal:

> They are thinking of doing away with our crossing lady and having a pelican crossing instead. Some of us don't like this idea.

Rewrite it in a more formal style.

Remember

Formal language is very **different** to how most people **speak normally**.

Personal because it uses the word 'we'

Here the **passive** voice is used. This removes the person from the sentence

Phrases like this can be used so that the view does not seem personal

---

Writing different text types

Writing instructions

The **purpose** of **instructions** is to tell the reader **how to do something**. You should think through the activity before you start writing and break the process up into a **sequence of clear steps**.

The instructions should be **clear** and **easy to follow**. Think particularly about the points where the readers might become confused or go wrong and make sure you give enough **detail** to help them through these difficulties.

Some hints

Here are eight points to remember when writing instructions:

- Make your **title** show the **purpose of the instructions**, for example:

   How to use your mobile phone

   How to play non-stop cricket

- Include an **introductory sentence** to make the task sound **appealing or useful**, for example:

   These biscuits are delicious and only take ten minutes to make.

- Give a list of items needed at the start, for example:

   Equipment: coloured card, pencil, ruler, scissors, glue

- Use short imperative sentences where possible. (Don't make the mistake of recounting what **you** did.) For example:

   Glue the shapes onto the box. ✓
   (**Not**: We glued the shapes... ✗)

   Divide the players into two teams. ✓
   (**Not**: We divided into... ✗)

- Use **adjectives** and **adverbs** if they add **important details** to the instructions, for example:

   <u>Carefully</u> fold the <u>large</u> sheet of paper in half.

- Make the instructions **easy to follow** by presenting the series of steps as a **numbered list**, or you could use **bullet points** if there is a list of short points.

- Give the reader extra detail about **how, where, when** – for example:

   Using the masking tape...; ...with the wooden spoon **(how)**

   3cm from the edge of the card...; ...on the cooling tray **(where)**

   While the paint is still wet...; Once the biscuits are cool... **(when).**

- Include a **final statement** to complete your instructions, for example:

   Now you can sit back and enjoy your crunchy cookies.

Test yourself!

Rewrite these points so that they sound like instructions:

1 We took the first turning on the left.

2 The cake was ready when we looked. It was lovely and brown.

Remember

Ask yourself whether **the reader** will be able to **follow your instructions.**

Writing different text types

Writing recounts

The **purpose** of a **recount** of an event is to **tell the reader exactly what happened**. Recounts can vary. They can be **personal** recounts, where you are retelling your own personal experiences, or they may be **factual** recounts, where you are retelling a known event or incident.

Recounts also vary depending on the **audience**. You could be writing for one of many different types of audience, for example a close friend – or the general public! If you are writing a **diary** or a **journal**, you will be **your own audience**.

Some hints

Here are six points to remember when writing recounts:

- **Write an introduction that sets the scene.** Give important background information about **who**, **when**, **where**, and **why**, for example:

  On 3rd August 1492 Christopher Columbus set sail from Spain on a voyage of discovery. (Factual recount)

  Last week Class 6 went on a visit to Warwick Castle as part of their history project. (Personal recount)

- **Recount the main events in the order they happened.** Start a new paragraph for each new event. Try using time connectives to link the events together, for example:

  Next, Soon, Later, After, In due course, Meanwhile, Finally

- **Do not write about every event in detail.** Choose the most interesting and most important events and write about these. Miss out any boring, unimportant parts.

- **Add details that make the events come alive for your reader.** This can include description to help your reader picture the scene or share feelings about the events described, for example:

  For three weeks they sailed with no sight of land. The members of the crew were becoming ever more desperate and frightened… (Factual recount)

  The steps leading down to the dungeon were narrow and uneven. There was an unpleasant smell of dampness in the air. (Personal recount)

- **Include comments on events.** Remember to think about the audience and the type of recount. This will tell you what sort of comment is appropriate, for example:

  Columbus had proved the Earth was round and opened up a New World of discovery. (Factual recount)

  What an amazing experience! (Personal recount)

- Your **conclusion** should give a final comment on the events.

> You can read more about connectives on pages 38, 52, 53, 57, 63 and 68.

Test yourself!

Write an entry for a personal diary or journal. In it, recount the events of a particularly exciting day out.

Pay special attention to the opening lines of this diary or journal entry.

Remember

There are **different types** of recount – make sure you know **what sort** you are writing.

Writing different text types

Writing a report for a newspaper

The **purpose** of a **newspaper report** is to tell the reader about **an event**. Reports are similar to **recounts** in that they describe what happened. But they also have some special features of their own.

Newspaper reports often include a **comment on the events** such as a quotation (or quote) from someone actually involved, or comments **about the consequences** or **importance** of the events. If you are writing a newspaper report you also need to think about **grabbing the reader's attention** with an **exciting headline** or **interesting viewpoint** on the story.

Some hints

Here are six points to remember when writing a newspaper report:

- **Start with a headline that will grab the reader's attention** – maybe by sounding dramatic or amusing, for example:

  Forest fire inferno

  It's a sizzling summer scorcher!

- **Begin with an overview of the events**, summarised in the opening sentence, for example:

  The city centre was closed for two hours yesterday morning, when an accident caused traffic chaos in Manchester.

- **Give a chronological account of the main events**, using separate paragraphs to make each event clear.

- **Give precise information about the people involved** in the story, for example:

  Mrs Tagore, aged 76, was on her way to her daughter's house when the accident happened. Samantha Jones, who works at the school, was the first to notice that something was wrong.

  > This information is **embedded** into the sentence. This is a technique often used in newspaper reports

- **Include quotes from the people involved** or people who saw the events, for example:

  Mrs Tagore is said to be very relieved to be home.

  Mr Daniels said, 'I am very surprised about the decision. It seems most unfair.'

  > You can **use direct or reported speech**. A direct quote needs speech marks like this

- At the end of the report give a **final comment** that sums up the events or looks to what might happen next.

Test yourself!

Write the opening sentence for a newspaper report with the headline:

Forest fire inferno

Remember

Newspaper reports have their own **style** and **features**. Try to **copy these** in your own reports.

Writing different text types

Writing a report

The **purpose** of a **report** is to **present information** in an **organised way**. It is very important to organise all your information into **different sections** before you start writing.

Reports usually include **definitions**, **descriptions** and **factual information** about different aspects of the subject.

A report might be part of an **information book**, a **comic** or **magazine**, or be included in a **letter** or **presentation**.

Manchester United
The home ground
Famous players
Successful managers
Trophies
The future?

Some hints

Here are six points to remember when writing reports:

- **When planning your report, group all the information under sub-headings,** each representing a different aspect of the subject. Use these sub-headings in your report. For example, a report on a football club might have the sub-headings:

  The home ground, Famous players, Successful managers, Trophies…

- **Include a short introduction** that **introduces** and **defines** the subject of the report, for example:

  Penguins are large flightless birds.

  Manchester United is one of the most successful Premiership teams.

- **Include general comments** about the subject of your report and give **specific examples**:

  General: <u>Many penguins</u> build nests out of stones or sticks.

  Specific: <u>The Emperor penguin</u> does not make a nest but places the egg on top of the male penguin's feet.

- Include **factual and precise description** (**not** imaginative description). You should use appropriate technical terms, for example:

  Penguins have short, powerful wings and webbed feet to help them swim.

- **Vary your sentences.** Do not start every sentence with the subject, for example:

  ~~Penguins cannot fly. Penguins are good swimmers. Penguins…~~   ✗

  Penguins cannot fly but they are good swimmers. They…   ✓

- Use the **present tense** (unless you are writing a report about something in the past).

Test yourself!

You have been asked to write a report on **different uses of the computer**.

What **sub-headings** would you use?

Remember

Reports present information in an organised way. Sort information under sub-headings.

Writing different text types

Persuasive writing

The **purpose** of **persuasive writing** is to **put forward a point of view** and to **persuade the reader to agree with you**. Persuasive writing can be in many different forms, including letters, leaflets, brochures or flyers – advertisements are also an example of persuasive writing.

The most important thing when writing persuasively is to be **positive** and **sure that you are right**. Think of all the reasons you can to **support your opinion** and **argue against other views**. Also think about **how you get your message across** – use methods that help you sound persuasive.

Some hints

Here are six points to remember when writing persuasively:

- **Clearly introduce your point of view at the start**, for example:

  Mobile phones are essential in the twenty-first century.

  Schools throw away vast quantities of paper that should be recycled.

- **Include a series of points or reasons that support your point of view** – one point to each paragraph. Give examples that help to explain each point. You can introduce your examples with the words:

  For example… • For instance… • An example of this is…

- **Think about what others might say and argue back**, for example:

  Although some people might say…, really ….

  Some people believe…, but is this true?

- **Involve the readers** – make them think and draw them in to agreeing with you, for example:

  Can you really…?   Do you want…?

  Start today – set up a recycling box in **your** classroom.

- **Sound positive** – make it seem obvious that everyone should agree with you. Use words like:

  Of course… • Obviously… • Clearly…
  No wonder…. • Surely… • The truth is …
  Everyone wants…

- **Use exciting adjectives and superlatives**. Exaggerate – particularly when writing adverts, for example:

  The coolest trainers on the block!

  Dreamy, delicious, delightful desserts …

- **End by reinforcing your point of view**, perhaps with a **snappy slogan**, for example:

  Recycle today – don't throw it away!

Test yourself!

Rewrite this point so that it sounds more persuasive:

A mobile phone is quite useful if you are going to be late home.

Remember

Sound **persuasive**. Give good **reasons**, but always **present** them in a **persuasive way**.

Writing different text types

Writing a balanced discussion

The **purpose** of a **balanced discussion** is to present **different points of view** on an issue. You might have your own **opinion**, but if you are writing a **discussion**, you must present **both sides of the argument**.

Think of discussions you see on television, where people put forward different views on an issue. What would the different members of the audience say about the issue you are writing on?

At the end of your discussion, you might be asked to come to a **conclusion**, or it might be left to the readers to make up their own minds.

Some hints

Here are six points to remember when writing a balanced discussion:

- **Introduce the issue in the title** – by posing a question, for example:

  Mobile phones – Love them or hate them?

  Are footballers paid too much?

- **Explain the issue and the different points of view** in your introduction, for example:

  Premiership footballers receive huge salaries. Some people believe that this is a fair reward for their skills, talent and hard work. Others feel that they do not deserve this amount of money.

- **Present the arguments for each point of view in turn**. Use a new paragraph for each new point. Link your points using connectives, such as:

  Firstly • Moreover • Furthermore
  However • On the other hand

- **Balance the different opinions** that are held on the subject, for example:

  While some people cannot live without their mobile phones, others really can't stand them.

- **Do not become personally involved** in the argument. Rather than using the words 'I think...', use phrases such as:

  Some people say... • Many people believe...
  It is known that...

- **End by summarising the different points of view**. If required, you can say which seems to offer the best argument, explaining why you came to that decision. For example:

  It would seem that overall... • All things considered ...

Test yourself!

Here is one point of view in a discussion about building a ring road:

> If the ring road were built, the tourist traffic would no longer need to go through the town centre. The streets would no longer be congested.

Write the opening sentence for the next paragraph, putting the **opposite point of view**, held by the shopkeepers in the town centre.

Remember

In a balanced discussion you must **present both sides fairly** – not just say what you think.

A checklist for writing

As you will have noticed, there is a lot to think about when you are writing, whether it is a story or non-fiction. The most important thing is to think about exactly **what** you are being asked to write and start from there. Then it is always a good idea to think of some **similar examples** that you have read and **use ideas from these** in your own writing.

Here is a checklist that you can use to remind you of some of the most important things to think about at different stages in your writing.

The checklist is divided into three parts, so that you can check separately what you need to do before, during and after you write.

Before you begin writing

- Make sure you know exactly **what** you are being asked to write and **who** will read it
- Work from the **ideas in the task** and think of ways you can **develop** them
- **Organise** your ideas. Make a **plan**

As you write

- Keep the **reader** and **purpose** in mind at all times so that you use the right **style** and **language**
- Think carefully about the **words** you use – don't write the first thing that comes into your head
- Think and write in **sentences**
- Use **different sorts of sentences**
- Use **paragraphs** to show that you have **organised** your ideas

When you have finished

- **Read through** what you have written
- Check that **everything makes sense**
- Add any **missing punctuation**

Test yourself!

Use this checklist to help you think about your own writing.

Is there something you have a particular problem with?

If so, work on improving it.

Use the Contents list or the Index to find the pages that will help you.

Remember

Use this three-part checklist to **plan** and **check** your own writing. **Keep it beside you when you write.**

Adjectives

An **adjective** is a **describing word**. An adjective is used to give additional information about a **noun**.

When you are **reading**, look out for adjectives, as they will help you to picture **settings**, **characters** and **events** described by the author.

When you are **writing**, use adjectives to help you make your **descriptions** more **interesting** and **accurate**.

Why are adjectives important?

Adjectives are very important words. Picture the scenes described below, and you will notice that the adjectives are the key words that make the three pictures different.

Kyle looked up at the sky.

Kyle looked up at the <u>angry</u> sky. It was <u>grey</u> and <u>threatening</u>.

Kyle looked up at the <u>glorious</u> sky. It was <u>blue</u> and <u>shimmering</u>.

How to choose adjectives

Because adjectives are important, you should choose them carefully. Avoid boring words that we use all the time, such as 'good' and 'nice'. Choose the most interesting and most descriptive words you can think of, for example:

He had a ~~nice~~ face. ✗   He had a <u>pleasant, friendly</u> face. ✓

How many adjectives should you use with one noun?

Don't use too many! Long lists of adjectives sound awkward, as in this example:

He took one step along the narrow, thin, dark and scary path. ✗

> Decide what is the most important feature – such as the darkness of the path

Sometimes you can replace a list of adjectives with one more carefully chosen noun, for example:

The small, grey furry animal sat under the tree... ✗

The squirrel sat under the tree ✓

Using adjectives in non-fiction writing

Adjectives are used less frequently in non-fiction writing. But they can help make writing more precise, as in these instructions:

Take the <u>blue</u> paper and cut a <u>small round</u> hole in the centre.

Test yourself!

Improve these sentences by adding adjectives (or choosing a better noun). Try to make each sentence create a picture in your head.

1 The child walked down the street.

2 The children came to a house.

3 The man watched the sea.

Remember

Adjectives help the reader to **picture** scenes. Use them to **create pictures** in your writing.

Adverbs

An **adverb** gives **additional information** about what is happening, for example, it will tell you **how**, **when** or **where** an event takes place. It is called an **ad**verb because it **adds** to the information that you are already given.

Look out for adverbs as you **read**, because they give **important clues** about **events**. They also tell you more about the **behaviour**, **feelings** and **thoughts** of the **characters** and the **author**. When you **write**, use adverbs to give **more detail** about what is happening.

Adding information with an adverb

The following examples show how an adverb adds **information** to a sentence:

She picked up the box.

She picked up the box <u>carefully</u>. (**how** it was done)

She picked up the box <u>yesterday</u>. (**when** it was done)

She picked up the box <u>outside</u>. (**where** it was done)

Where to place an adverb

One of the great things about adverbs is that they can be moved around in a sentence, for example:

She picked up the box carefully.

She carefully picked up the box.

Carefully, she picked up the box.

> Notice that placing the adverb at the **start** of the sentence puts more emphasis on **how** she picked up the box, rather than the action itself

This is a useful **technique** to use when you are writing. Try putting an adverb in different places and decide which version of the sentence sounds best.

Should you use an adverb – or a more powerful verb?

Only use adverbs when they are really needed. Sometimes it is better to choose a **more powerful verb**, for example:

He ~~walked slowly~~ down the road. ✗

He sauntered/ ambled/ strolled down the road. ✓

Using adverbs in non-fiction writing

In non-fiction texts, adverbs can give an author's comment on the events being described:

The discovery <u>unfortunately</u> came too late.

Test yourself!

Find the two adverbs in this description:

Jade carefully lifted the latch and quietly slipped through the gate.

Remember

Adverbs give added information about events.

Pronouns

A **pronoun** is a word used **in place of** a **noun**. The pronouns we use most often are **personal pronouns**, such as **I, she, he, her, us, it**. Using pronouns means that you do not need to keep repeating the same names or words throughout a text.

When you are **reading**, look out for pronouns and make sure that you know **which character**, or **what**, they are referring to. When you are **writing**, use pronouns to **avoid repeating yourself**. But be careful – **too many pronouns** and your reader will become **confused**.

Use pronouns to avoid repetition

Here is an example that shows why pronouns are used:

Without pronouns: Jim used Jim's mobile phone to call Jim's father.
With pronouns: Jim used his mobile phone to call his father.

Without pronouns, the writer had to keep on repeating Jim's name.

Use pronouns to make links

Pronouns can be used to make links between sentences, for example:

Indira decided to stay on the beach. It was not a good idea as she soon discovered.

> 'It' means the decision to stay on the beach, mentioned in the first sentence

In this example, the second sentence would not make sense without the first. This is important when reading. You must make sure that you know which character or event is being referred to. This might mean going back and reading the previous sentence or paragraph if you need to. For example:

That seemed like a good idea to her.

| What? | | Who? |

Here you would need to go back and read the previous sentence or paragraph to find out what was being referred to.

Don't use too many pronouns!

When you are writing, make sure you don't use too many pronouns, or your reader will become confused about what or who you are talking about. Always read through each paragraph to check that everything is clear.

Test yourself!

Rewrite these sentences using pronouns in place of some of the nouns:

Ali put the hat on. The hat was too big and fell over Ali's eyes. The hat can't be Ali's thought Ali. The hat must be Ed's.

Remember

Too many pronouns and your reader will become **confused**. **Too few** and writing sounds **repetitive**.

Connectives

A **connective** is a word or phrase that **makes links** between ideas in a text. A link is like one part of a chain. Some connectives link ideas **within a sentence** (these are called **conjunctions**). Other connectives make links **between different sentences, paragraphs** or **parts** of a text.

When **reading** it is important to pay attention to connectives as they tell you how events, facts or pieces of information **relate to each other**. When **writing**, it is important to use a **range of different** connectives to help link your ideas together.

Different types of connectives make links in different ways. See below for some examples.

Time connectives

These show the time relationship between events, for example:

Just then ● Later ● In the end ● Afterwards
Before ● Until then ● Meanwhile ● Earlier
Prior to this ● At the same time

Time connectives are found in stories, recounts and some explanations.

Cause and effect connectives

These show how one event causes or results in something else happening, for example:

Consequently ● As a result
Therefore ● Because ● As ● Since

Cause and effect connectives are found in reports, explanations, persuasive texts and discussions.

Contrasting or balancing connectives

These are used when presenting an idea that is different to what has gone before, for example:

However ● In contrast ● Whereas
On the other hand ● Although ● Despite this

Contrasting or balancing connectives are found in discussions and persuasive texts.

You can read more about connectives on pages 38, 52, 53, 57, 59 and 63.

Test yourself!

Choose a connective from the white box to link these two ideas:

Mobile phones can be very useful.

Some people find them annoying.

| Later   Therefore   However |

Remember

Use **connectives** in your writing to show **how** your ideas **link together**.

Writing in sentences

Thinking in sentences

When we write, we write in **sentences**. So whenever you are writing, it is a good idea to **think in sentences**. In other words, **compose each sentence in your head** before you write it down.

Trying out sentences like this means that you can **try out different versions of the sentence** and **see which sounds best**. Another benefit of thinking in sentences is that it helps you to remember **capital letters at the start** of sentences and **full stops at the end**.

Simple sentences

Here are some examples of simple sentences. Notice that all sentences, no matter how short, must include a verb, start with a **capital letter** and end with a **full stop**:

He waited.

The ground shook.

The forest was ablaze.

Very short sentences like these can be used to create **impact** in writing. They stand out because they are so short.

Compound sentences

Sometimes two sentences are joined together using the words **and** or **but**. These are called compound sentences, for example:

He was late. He missed the bus. ➜ He was late and he missed the bus.

She shouted and shouted. No one heard. ➜ She shouted and shouted but no one heard.

A common mistake to avoid

A common mistake is to use **commas** to separate sentences, rather than **full stops**. For example:

She shouted and shouted but no one heard, perhaps there was no one left to hear, the silence closed in around her. ✗

This is wrong. **Full stops** are needed here, **not commas**, to separate the three sentences.

Test yourself!

Complete these two compound sentences:

1 He missed the bus but

2 She shouted and shouted and

Remember

Try out sentences **in your head** before you write them down.

Sentence types

There are a number of **different forms** of sentence, for example:

- statements
- questions
- commands or instructions
- exclamations.

Using different types of sentence can help to bring **variety** to your writing. Here are some examples of the different types.

Statements

These two examples are straightforward statements:

The day was cold.

Charles Dickens was born in 1812.

Questions

As well as asking for information, questions can also be used in both fiction and non-fiction writing to draw the reader in and make them think about the subject or event.

Who had been outside the window? Whose footprints were they?

Do you believe there is life on other planets?

Would you like to be a grand prix driver?

Commands or instructions

Commands and instructions speak directly to the reader. They are used in many non-fiction texts, not just when writing instructions.

Visit the greatest show on Earth.

Try out these tricks on your friends.

Have fun.

Exclamations

Exclamations tend to be short and to the point. They are good for grabbing the reader's attention.

What a surprise!

That's amazing!

Test yourself!

Here is a statement about a new variety of ice cream.

It is made with real fruit.

Write a **question**, a **command** and an **exclamation** that you could use in an advertisement for this ice cream.

Remember

Use **different types** of **sentence** to help make your writing more **effective**.

Complex sentences

A **complex** sentence has more than one part or clause – a **main clause** that makes sense on its own and a **subordinate clause** that does not. Complex sentences are used because they **make links between ideas** and help to **express ideas** neatly. They also make writing sound more **flowing**, more **formal** and more **grown-up**.

You will find complex sentences in both fiction and non-fiction texts. Learning how to use them in your own writing will help you to **put across your ideas** and to **improve the style and sound** of your writing.

Comparing simple and complex sentences

Here is part of a story written in simple sentences:

Abby followed the path. She came to some gates. She paused there.

She did not know what to do. The gates were tall and padlocked.

The use of short simple sentences makes the story sound jerky. Here is the same idea, rewritten using **complex** sentences:

Abby followed the path until she came to some gates. She paused there, not knowing what to do, as the gates were tall and padlocked.

Using conjunctions to make complex sentences

Words like **until** and **as** can be used to **link clauses together**. These are called **conjunctions**. Here are some other conjunctions you can use to link ideas together in complex sentences.

after ● as ● although ● before ● because
despite ● if ● since ● so ● unless
until ● when ● while

These words can also be used in writing to form sentences that link together pieces of information, for example:

Separate simple sentences:
The houses were made of wood. The fire spread quickly.

One complex sentence:
As the houses were made of wood, the fire spread quickly.

Separate simple sentences:
Bake the biscuits in the oven. Take them out when they are brown.

One complex sentence:
Bake the biscuits in the oven until they are brown.

Test yourself!

Choose a conjunction from the box to link these two pieces of information into one sentence:

The fire-fighters continued to fight the blaze _____ they were exhausted.

| because if although |
| as since |

Remember

Use complex sentences in your own writing.

Complex sentences

Starting sentences with a subordinate clause

Complex sentences can be **reordered**. The subordinate or extra clause can be placed at the **start** or **end** of a sentence. A subordinate clause gives you **more information** about the **main clause**.

Starting with a subordinate clause is a useful technique in both fiction and non-fiction writing, as it adds **variety** to your sentences. It also means that you are more likely to **notice** the information given in the subordinate clause. When you are writing, **try out** complex sentences **in your head**. Think about **different ways of forming the sentence** and decide which version sounds best.

In fiction writing

In fiction, a subordinate clause at the start of a sentence can suggest a character's motives or feelings, for example:

When the rain stopped, he went into the garden.

As the clock struck twelve, he went into the garden.

Despite his fears, he went into the garden.

When the subordinate clause is put at the start of the sentence, a comma is needed to separate it from the main clause	The main clause

You do not always have to use a conjunction to start the sentence. You can start with a verb, for example:

<u>Whistling</u> happily to himself, he went into the garden.

<u>Hearing</u> the alarm, he went into the garden.

<u>Muttering</u> angrily, he went into the garden.

In non-fiction writing

In non-fiction texts, starting with a subordinate clause is a useful technique for providing variety and changing the focus of a sentence:

Despite his many achievements, he died penniless.

If you leave it too long, the paint will dry.

Annoyed by the decision, he resigned immediately.

Test yourself!

Add to the start of these sentences a subordinate clause that suggests the feelings of the characters.

1 She stepped onto the stage.

2 He climbed down.

Remember

Sometimes, **start** a sentence with a **subordinate clause**.

Complex sentences

Embedding information

You can also add a subordinate clause or an extra piece of information into the **middle** of the main sentence. This is called '**embedding**', and is often used in journalistic writing, such as newspaper reports.

This technique works best when the **subordinate clause** or extra information is quite **short**, otherwise the final sentence can sound clumsy. You should try out the sentence in your head first, to see how it sounds.

Some examples from fiction

> This is the **main sentence**. The extra information has been placed in the middle

Yasmin, her hands shaking, opened the box.

Kyle, who knew this was his last chance, took a deep breath.

The dragon, breathing plumes of smoke, opened his leathery wings.

> Notice that two **commas** are used to mark the **start** and **end** of the subordinate clause

Some examples from non-fiction

Polar bears, **having yellowish-white fur**, are well camouflaged in Arctic conditions.

Bears, **when hungry or annoyed**, have been known to attack humans.

Other short pieces of information, such as definitions, can be embedded into a sentence in the same way. For example:

Bears are carnivorous, **or meat-eating**, animals.

Test yourself!

Add the extra information into the main sentence.

Main sentence: The dog was desperate to escape.
Extra information: The dog was barking madly.

Remember

You can add a **short phrase** or **clause** into the **middle** of a sentence.

Punctuation

Punctuation is important because it helps the reader to **follow the meaning** of a piece of writing. You should always pay attention to the punctuation when reading. It will help you to make sense of the **meaning** of text, and will also give you **clues** about how the text should **sound** when it is **read aloud**.

When you are writing, it is important to make sure that you use punctuation correctly so that your reader reads the text exactly as you hear it in your head.

An example from a fiction text

All the punctuation has been removed from the fiction text quoted below.

> Jade brown are you with us mrs Andersons
> voice cut into my comfortable dream world it
> was a hot afternoon too hot for history projects

The text is difficult to read because you do not know **where to pause** or what **expression** to use. We don't know how the author intended it to sound. If the whole story were written like this, it would be difficult to **follow what was happening**.

With punctuation, the extract might look like this:

> 'Jade Brown! Are you with us?' Mrs Anderson's
> voice cut into my comfortable dream world. It
> was a hot afternoon – too hot for history projects.

> The dash is used for effect

The punctuation makes the writing easier to read and more effective.

An example from a non-fiction text

Here is an extract of non-fiction writing, again without any punctuation:

> Ever dreamed of being a grand prix driver well heres your
> chance the new gp driver game puts you yes you behind the
> wheel its fast its furious its fun totally wicked

This is the same extract with punctuation:

> Ever dreamed of being a grand prix driver? Well, here's your
> chance. The new GP Driver game puts you – yes you! – behind
> the wheel. It's fast, it's furious, it's fun – totally wicked!

The punctuation helps to bring the text to life and gets across the style and sound that the writer intended.

Test yourself!

Put punctuation into this diary extract so that it makes sense and sounds more effective:

> dad was not pleased
> well would you be hed
> been stuck in the house
> all day looking after a
> sick cat angry he was
> positively fuming

Remember

Punctuation is **vital** when reading and writing – **don't ignore it.**

Sentence punctuation

When we write, we write in **sentences**. The **start** and **end** of each sentence must be clearly shown with a **capital letter** and a **full stop** (or a **question mark** or **exclamation mark** if needed). If you **think** in sentences as you write, you will get into the habit of **using** sentence punctuation as you go.

If you have forgotten to mark the start and end of sentences, it is important to proof read your writing. When checking sentence punctuation it is best to **read aloud in your head**, so that you can hear where each sentence ends.

Capital letters are used at the start of all types of sentence. Capital letters are also used for:

- names of people, places
- titles, e.g. Miss
- the days of the week, months of the year
- to make a word stand out, e.g. HELP!

Some examples of sentence punctuation

The water comes rushing down the mountainside. It carries with it stones and rocks.

| Capital letters are used to show the start of each sentence | Full stops to show the end of each sentence |

Sometimes a question mark or exclamation mark is needed instead of a full stop. For example:

You might have seen pictures of strange patterns made in fields of wheat or corn. These patterns are called crop circles. But how do they get there? Let's investigate!

| This sentence asks a question, so a question mark is used rather than a full stop | The writer wanted to make this sound exciting, so has used an exclamation mark rather than a full stop |

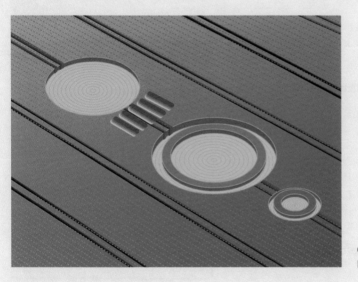

Crop circles in the fields near Winterford Hill (viewed from an aircraft)

Test yourself!

Proof read this extract. Put in the missing sentence punctuation:

Many people keep animals as pets cats and dogs are particularly popular other people prefer smaller animals such as gerbils or hamsters

Remember

Read your writing **aloud in your head** when **checking sentence punctuation**.

Commas

Commas are used **within** a sentence. They show the **breaks** between **different parts** of the sentence. Understanding how commas work will help you to make sense of complex sentences that you meet when reading.

When to use commas – some hints

As a writer, you need to learn how to use commas to separate parts of sentences. When should you use them? The examples below will give you some hints.

To separate items in a list

For example:

In the wooden box there was an old-fashioned fountain pen, some coins, a matchbox and a folded piece of paper.

After connecting words and phrases that start a sentence

For example:

After a long time, they came to the end of the tunnel.

However, this is not always true.

> **Never** use commas **between sentences** – always use **full stops**.

To separate a phrase or clause that is embedded into a sentence

For example:

Mr Khan, a former pilot, admitted that he was a reluctant hero.

The kitten, purring softly, brushed against my legs.

Test yourself!

Put at least one comma into each of these sentences:

1 Mr Roberts my teacher is very strange.

2 First sieve the flour into the bowl.

3 Although it was very late we were wide awake.

Between clauses in a complex sentence

Commas used between clauses are used to separate the main clause and the subordinate clause, for example:

While the dough is rising, heat the oven to the correct temperature.

Smiling nervously, she opened the door.

She opened the door, smiling nervously.

Remember

Commas are used **within** a sentence to **separate** the **different parts**.

Dashes and brackets

Dashes and **brackets** are both used when **adding extra information** into a sentence.

Using dashes

Dashes can be used on their **own** or in **pairs**. They are often used **for effect** in **informal** writing and stories.

One dash

A single dash can be used to add extra information to the end of a sentence:

> Dad cooked us a meal – it was terrible!

A dash at the end of a sentence is often used for effect, as it helps to create a dramatic pause:

> I tried the key in the lock – it worked!

> I was quietly watching TV when – CRASH!

Two dashes

A pair of dashes can be used to embed the extra information into the middle of a sentence:

> The twins – as always – were late.

Using brackets

Brackets are always used as a **pair**. They add extra information into a sentence, and this information is cut off from the main sentence. They can be useful in both **formal** and **informal** writing. For example:

> The twins (Lloyd and Des) were late.

> I wrote a letter of complaint to Mr Manson (the manager).

> Double click on the icon on the tool bar (see diagram).

Sometimes a whole sentence can be put into brackets, as shown below:

> Use sharp scissors to cut out the centre of the shape. (Ask an adult to help you.)

Test yourself!

Add dashes or brackets to these sentences:

1 He made it to the bus stop just as the bus pulled out.

2 For dinner there was shepherd's pie yuk! and sprouts double yuk.

Remember

Dashes and **brackets** are used to **add extra information** into a sentence.

Colons and semi-colons

Colons and **semi-colons** are more **complex** punctuation marks. They are usually only found in texts aimed at **older readers** or an adult audience. Colons and semi-colons tend to be used more in **formal writing**. In informal writing, a dash is sometimes used instead.

Using colons and semi-colons in your writing can add **style** and make your writing seem more **mature** and more **formal**.

Here are some examples to show how colons and semi-colons are used.

Using colons

You can use a colon to:

- **Introduce a list**

  For his lunch, he had: two pitta breads, a slice of cake, crisps and an apple.

- **Introduce a quotation**

  The writer says: 'Travelling beyond the Solar System is not possible.'

- **Introduce a second part of the sentence**

  It was too late: the tide had turned.

  > This second part of the sentence usually explains or illustrates the first part of the sentence.

Using semi-colons

You can use a semi-colon:

- **In place of a connective between two linked main clauses**

  The lamb struggled to its feet; it seemed determined to survive.

- **In a list made up of longer phrases**

  The mouse had tiny, beady eyes; perfectly-formed pink ears; curiously twitching whiskers and a most inquisitive look.

  > Here, two semi-colons separate out the different items in the list.

Test yourself!

Rewrite these sentences with the correct punctuation. Use a colon or semi-colon in each sentence:

1 Then the announcement came 'We regret that this flight is cancelled'.

2 The door opened a strange man peered at me.

Remember

Use **colons** and **semi-colons** to form **complex sentences**.

Learning to spell

Knowing **how to spell** is important. Correctly spelled words make your writing easier to read. Being able to spell words easily also allows you more time to think about **what** you are writing, rather than **how** you spell it. Therefore it is especially important that you learn to spell words that you often use in your writing.

Learning to spell a word means **looking at it very carefully**, finding **patterns** or **focusing on the tricky part**. It can sometimes help to **write the word down** a number of times, or to **say the word how it is spelt**. You can even use a mnemonic to help you. Some examples of these methods are shown below. Try them all and see what works best for you.

Remember

When you are learning to spell a word:

Look ● Cover ● Write ● Check

Always check that a word looks right when you have written it.

Looking at words carefully

- **Look**
  Try looking at words carefully and highlighting the part you usually get wrong. This is the part of the word you must focus on. For example:

  colour ● laughter ● guilty

- **Cover**
  Cover the word up. Try to remember how to spell it.

- **Write**
  While the word is still covered up, see if you can write it. Think about whether the word looks right as you have spelled it.

- **Check**
  Uncover the correctly-spelled word. Check whether you spelled it right.

Finding patterns

When you are learning to spell a word, it can be useful to learn at the same time any **other words** that follow a **similar pattern**. For example:

light ● might ● night ● fight
flight ● fright ● slight
usual ● actual ● casual ● manual

Test yourself!

Write down the correct spelling of **five words** that you find difficult.

Use the ideas on this page to help you learn how to spell these five words.

Test yourself to see if you can remember them.

Using a mnemonic

You might find that a mnemonic helps you to remember the **tricky part** of a spelling. Here are some mnemonics that might help you:

- **because**: **b**ig **e**lephants **c**an **a**lways **u**nderstand **s**mall **e**lephants → **because**
- **cemetery**: all the vowels in the cemetery are 'e's
- **pieces**: see the **pie** in **pieces**

Breaking words into syllables

Breaking longer words into syllables is especially useful when you are trying to **spell them**, because this helps you to:

- **think about each part of the word** separately, rather than the whole word together
- **find 'words within words'** – these are smaller words within the longer word, and they help you to remember the correct spelling
- **find hidden letters** – these are letters that are difficult to hear when the word is said normally. They are sometimes called **unstressed letters** and they often cause spelling problems.

Thinking about each part of the word

The words below are easier to spell when you break them into syllables:

re/mem/ber/ing   ●   un/der/stand
af/ter/noon   ●   dis/tur/bing

Finding words within words

Sometimes when you break words up into syllables, you will find words within words. These can help you remember how to spell the longer words. For example:

main/ten/ance   ●   de/**pen/dent**

Finding hidden letters

Breaking words up into syllables can help you find hidden or unstressed letters. For example:

math/**e**/mat/ics   ●   choc/**o**/late
dif/**fer**/ent   ●   gov/**ern**/ment

You can learn how to spell these words by saying them **as they are written**, rather than **how they usually sound**. Say them so that you notice the sound of the hidden letter. Here are some more examples:

Wed/**nes**/day   ●   Feb/**ru**/ary
in/**ter**/est/ing   ●   mis/**er**/able

> When you say these words normally, you do not notice the letters shown in bold print

Test yourself!

Break these words up into syllables and underline the letter that is not clear when you just say the word normally:

1 desperate

2 family

3 predict

Remember

Look out for **letters that are difficult to hear** when you say the word normally.

Root words, prefixes and suffixes

A **prefix** or **suffix** can be added to a **root word** to make a **new word**.

Prefixes

A **prefix** is added to the **beginning** of a word:

- it **does not** change the **spelling** of the root word
- it **does** change the **meaning** of the root word.

Here are some examples:

- mis + understood = misunderstood
- un + happy = unhappy
- dis + appear = disappear
- il + logical = illogical
- al + together = altogether | Notice that the prefix is **al** rather than **all** |

Suffixes

A **suffix** is added to the **end** of a word:

- it **sometimes** changes the **spelling** of the root word (if it normally ends with 'e' or 'y')
- it **always** changes the **meaning** of the root word.

Note that the spelling of the root word only changes sometimes. Usually it does not change, for example:

- friend + ly = friendly
- colour + ful = colourful | Notice that the suffix is spelt **ful**, not **full** |
- govern + ment = government
- hero + ic = heroic
- invent + ive = inventive
- kind + ness = kindness

Remember the special rules below. They explain when and how the spelling of a root word can change when you add a suffix.

When the root word ends with 'e'

If the suffix starts with a **vowel**, **drop** the 'e', for example:

love + **able** = lovable

If the suffix starts with a **consonant**, **keep** the 'e', for example:

love + **ly** = lovely

When the root word ends with a consonant followed by a 'y'

You usually change the 'y' to an 'i', for example:

happy + ness = happiness
happy + ly = happily
happy + er = happier

Test yourself!

Add these suffixes and prefixes to the root words:

1 beauty + ful =

2 heavy + er =

3 arrive + al =

4 dis + honest =

5 im + mature =

6 un + comfortable =

Remember

Make sure you know the rules for adding suffixes.

Verb and plural endings

Verb endings

The word endings that we add most often are the verb endings -ing and -ed. In most cases, adding them is straightforward. You just add the ending, for example:

jump   jumping   jumped

There are some rules to remember if the verb ends with 'y' or 'e'. There are also some occasions when the last letter needs to be doubled. Read and learn the rules below.

If the verb ends with 'e'

Drop the 'e' to add -ing and -ed, for example:
hope   hoping   hoped

If the verb ends in a short vowel followed by a consonant

Double the last letter when adding -ing and -ed, for example:
hop   hopping   hopped

If the verb ends with a consonant followed by 'y'

When adding -ed, change the 'y' to an 'i', for example:
hurry   hurried

When adding -ing, keep the 'y', for example:
hurry   hurrying

Plural endings

Most words can be made into plurals by adding 's', for example:

cakes   girls   books   boys

Some words change their spelling when the 's' is added. Here are some rules – make sure that you know them!

If a word ends with a hissing or buzzing sound (s, ch, sh, x)

Add -es, for example:
classes   catches   wishes   boxes

If a word ends with a consonant followed by 'y'

Drop the 'y' and add -ies, for example:
lady → ladies   diary → diaries   party → parties

If a word ends with 'f' or -fe

Drop the 'f'/-fe and add –ves, for example:
knife → knives   life → lives   half → halves

Test yourself!

Use the rules to help you add -ed and -ing to these verbs:

1 worry

2 smile

3 hum

4 scream

Remember

Remember the rules for adding -s, -ing and -ed.

More spelling rules

Spelling rules are useful because they **help you** to spell lots of words **correctly**. Here are **three more spelling rules** for you to remember:

- 'i' before 'e' except after 'c'
- the letter 'q' is always followed by a 'u' (and another vowel)
- no words in English end with the letter 'v' (unless they are shortened forms).

Let's look at some examples that will help you to understand these rules.

'i' before 'e' except after 'c'

This rule only works if the 'i' and 'e' together make a long 'ee' sound, for example:

i before e	except after c
thief	ceiling
niece	receipt
fierce	receive

Words where there is no long 'ee' sound do not follow the rule, for example:

eight • their • weigh

The letter 'q' is always followed by a 'u' (and another vowel)

quaint • qualify • quarrel • quarter
question • quick • quilt • quotation

No English words end with the letter v ...

... so if you hear a 'v' sound at the end of a word, it must end 've'.

forgive • nerve • twelve • attractive

It is also unusual to find the letter 'j' at the end of English words. Words that end with this sound are usually spelt -ge or -dge.

huge • cage
wage • edge
bridge • fudge

Test yourself!

Use the rules to help you choose the correct spelling of these words:

1 sqiurrel squirrel sqirrel

2 depriv depriyv deprive

3 belief beleef beleif

Remember

Learning a **spelling rule** will help you to spell **lots of words correctly**.

Difficult letters

Letters can make **different sounds** in **different words**. Some letters have two sounds – a **hard** sound and a **soft** sound. The letters 'c' and 'g' are both examples of letters with two sounds.

There are other letters that sometimes make **no sound at all**. We call these **silent** letters.

It is a good idea to be aware of these tricky letters when making decisions about how to spell a word.

Letters with two sounds

The letter 'c' has two sounds

It usually makes a **hard** sound like the letter 'k', as in the words:

cat   custard   reclaim

But sometimes it makes a **soft** sound like the letter 's', as in the words:

cellar   bicycle   city

'c' usually makes a soft sound when it is followed by 'i', 'e' or 'y'

The letter 'g' has two sounds

It usually makes a **hard** sound, as in the words:

green   gold   angry   again   gulp

But sometimes it makes a **soft** sound like the letter 'j', as in the words:

general   giraffe   magic   gym

'g' often makes a soft sound when it is followed by 'i', 'e' or 'y'

Silent letters

Some letters can be silent – sometimes they make no sound at all, for example:

- Silent 'k': knife   knee   knock   knitting
- Silent 'w': write   wrong   wrist   wreck
- Silent 'b': bomb   comb   limb

Test yourself!

Complete these words by adding the letter 'c' or 's'.

Remember that 'c' makes a **soft sound** if followed by 'i', 'e' or 'y'.

1 _avage

2 _eiling

3 _inema

4 _olid

5 _ylinder

Remember

The letters 'c' and 'g' only make a **soft sound** if followed by 'i', 'e' or 'y'.

Homophones and other tricky words

Homophones

Homophones are words that **sound the same** but are **spelt differently** and have **different meanings**. When you write down a homophone, you need to decide which version of the word is needed.

The following homophones are especially confusing:

- peace (peace and quiet)   piece (piece of paper)
- right (right and wrong)   write (write it down)
- stair (sit on the stair)   stare (stand and stare)
- here (here and there)   hear (use your ear to hear)

> This will help you to get the right here/ hear

Here are some more homophones. Use a dictionary to check which spelling has which meaning:

- ate   eight
- bare   bear
- which   witch
- bean   been
- there   their
- thrown   throne
- waste   waist
- hole   whole
- pain   pane

Homographs

Homographs are words that look the same, because they have the **same spelling**, but have a number of **different meanings**. For example:

- club (a big stick)   club (a group of people)
- watch (to look at what happens)   watch (it tells you the time)
- wave (with your hand)   wave (on the sea)

Other tricky words

Other words that are difficult to spell are those with **unusual letter patterns** or **confusing groups of letters**. A mnemonic (such as a chant or a saying) can be useful to help you remember tricky words like these, for example:

- queue (say: que-ue)
- icicles (say: ic-ic-les)
- occasion (say: double 'c' but one 's')
- necessary (say: single 'c' but double 's')

Test yourself!

Write the second word in these pairs of homophones:

1 blue   and   _ _ _ _
2 break   and   _ _ _ _ _
3 cereal   and   _ _ _ _ _ _

Remember

Make sure you **write** the **right** homophone.

Handwriting

Your **handwriting** should usually be **joined up**. As well as looking neat, joined up handwriting is very useful when writing **quickly** or **at length**. Keep printed (capital) letters for headings or sub-headings.

The most important thing is that your handwriting is **clear**. Both the **letters** and the **joining lines between the letters** must be correctly formed. Other things that you should watch are the **size**, **spacing** and **slant** of your writing.

A handwriting checklist

Here are the four main things you should watch out for when you are practising your handwriting. Notice that they all begin with 's', which should help you to remember them.

Shape

Make sure that all your letters are **properly shaped** and **joined correctly**.

Size

Watch the size of **capital letters** and **tall letters** like 'h', 'k', 'l' and 'd'. Make sure that these are clearly **taller than the small letters** like 'a', 'c' and 'n'.

Make sure that all the **small letters** are the **same height**. It is easy to let the letter 's' in particular become too large if you are not careful.

Make sure that the **tail** on **descenders**, such as 'g', 'y' and 'p', is clearly **below the line** – but don't make it too long and straggly.

Spacing

Spaces between words should be the **same size**.

Watch the **spaces between letters**. Don't squash letters up, and don't leave huge spaces between letters either.

Slant

Make sure the slant of your writing **stays the same** through one piece of writing. All the letters should either go straight up or lean slightly in the same direction.

Watch particularly the slant on ascenders and descenders. It is easy to let some lean to the side while others go straight up or down.

Test yourself!

Practise your handwriting by writing a short paragraph of information about yourself.

Use the points on this page to help you judge your handwriting. Look for any problems. Then work on putting these problems right.

Remember

The four words beginning with 's':

Shape
Size
Spacing
Slant

Don't force your writing to lean over. You will lose the flow of your writing and it will look untidy.

Answers

Page 4
Set up your reading log as suggested.

Page 5

Jack climbs a beanstalk	2
Jack steals a magic hen	4
Jack exchanges his cow for beans	1
Jack chops down the beanstalk	5
Jack discovers a castle	3

Page 6
You should have referred to any four from:
- The author says Mrs Pringle is 'like a pillow – soft, comfortable and always there when needed'
- The children call her 'Granny Pringle'
- She is 'always there' for the children
- 'gentle words'
- 'cheery smile'

Page 7
The phrase 'a cold fist clenched in his stomach' shows that the character is frightened of going inside. He is trying to put off this moment, because he walked 'slowly' and he came to the gate 'all too quickly'. He looks around for things to distract him.

Page 8
You should mention some of these techniques used by the author:
- he gives details about the box, e.g. 'half-hidden', 'simple wooden'
- he makes it sound as if it has special powers ('draw him towards it')
- he makes the reader wonder about what is inside (e.g. it was 'surprisingly heavy', 'Perhaps there was something inside')
- he builds up to the moment when the box is opened – seeing it, describing it, picking it up.

Page 9
It is told in the first person, from the point of view of one of the ugly sisters.
The story is usually told in the third person, and from the point of view of Cinderella.
The effect is to make Cinderella seem less sympathetic in this version.

Page 10
The word 'precious' shows that the glimpse of the sky was very important to the prisoner. It was valuable because it provided his only bit of light and was his only reminder of the outside world.

Page 11
Simile: 'the cave was like a magnet to them'
The simile shows that the children were fascinated with the cave and could not keep away from it.

Page 12
- Characters are typically 'good' and 'bad'.
  The good character faces an enemy or a rival.
- Events are based around a central problem.
  There are lots of problems and dangers to overcome.
  There are twists and turns, surprises and suspense.
- Problems are usually solved at the end.
  The 'good' character usually comes out on top.

Page 13
That it is important to share things and not be greedy. If the brothers had agreed to share the chapatti in the first place, rather than each wanting it all, the stranger would not have been able to trick them.

Page 14
Something dark and sinister would fit with the mood of the stories. Shadowy, rather than clear, illustrations would **suggest** what was there, rather than **showing** it.

Page 15
It does not matter if you answered yes or no. The important thing is the reasons you give for your opinion.
Make sure that you have given three reasons why you liked/disliked the story.
You should have supported each of your reasons by referring to the text. So if you have said that the story was exciting, make sure you have given an example of an exciting part.

Page 16
Make sure that you have written down your first thoughts and feelings.

Page 17
You should have referred to the lines:
'The cruel crawling foam,
The cruel hungry foam'

Page 18
He uses the word 'wrinkled' because it describes the ripples and waves on the surface of the sea as seen from high up.

Page 19
The simile describes the power and sudden movement of the eagle as it dives down. It also helps to suggest the deadly result of the eagle swooping on its unsuspecting prey.

Page 20
Rhyme – all the lines have the same rhyme (hands, lands, stands).
Rhythm – four strong stresses in each line.
Alliteration – 'clasps the crag with crooked hands', 'lonely lands'.

Answers

Page 21
The first, second and fifth lines rhyme (Fred, bed, fed).
The third and fourth lines rhyme (way, day).
The rhythm of lines three and four is different to the rest of the poem. (There are three stresses in lines 1, 2 and 5, and just two stresses in lines 3 and 4.)

Page 22
…for example, the writer describes the water as 'calm and still'.

Page 23
- Look at the Contents page. Note that the information is organised into sections. There are sections on **reading** fiction, poetry and non-fiction and sections on **writing** fiction and non-fiction. There are also sections on spelling, punctuation and grammar.
- You should have used the page headings as well as the Contents page to get an overview of the content and organisation.

Page 24
The fifth planet is Jupiter.
Pluto is described as 'rocky' and 'icy'.

Page 25
Mercury – closest to the Sun, small and rocky, 88 days.
Pluto – furthest from the Sun, rocky but icy, 248 years.

Page 26
Answers should refer to the strength or power of the elephant and how this would be useful for moving tree trunks or carrying heavy loads.

Page 27
1 Report
2 Instructions
3 Recount

Page 28
1 A list is easy for the readers to refer to as they collect the items they need.
2 The numbers show the order in which the reader should follow the points.
3 The diagrams will help to make clear some of the more difficult steps.

Page 29
The photograph might make the readers feel sorry for the puppy, so that they are more likely to give money to the shelter.

Page 30
'the best current writer of realistic stories' is an opinion held by the author; it cannot be proved to be a fact.

Page 31
The quote is from someone who knows about fires and gives an expert's explanation of the conditions.
The quote also looks at the story from a different angle – it shows the role of the fire-fighters in putting out the blaze.

Page 32
This amusing comment is used to sum up the information just given about Tyrannosaurus Rex, e.g. it can open its mouth very wide, it can eat huge quantities of meat in one bite, it is always hunting for food.
(It is not enough to say that the phrase is amusing without relating it to the information about the dinosaur.)

Page 33
It does not matter which word you chose. The important thing is that you explain your choice by referring to specific aspects of the text.
For example, point out techniques the writer used to make it interesting or easy to use, explain how it was useful for a specific task, or what aspects you found confusing.

Page 34
I thought this new computer game was great, until suddenly something strange happened. This was the start of an amazing adventure…

Page 35
1 It is an adventure story with some parts being realistic and some parts being fantasy.
2 It is told in the first person from the point of view of the main character (the person playing the computer game).

Page 36
This is an example of the sort of notes you should have made:

Characters
- Sharnie – girl – loves computer games
- Mikey – her brother – annoying
- The Empress – character in a computer game – evil

Setting
- Sharnie's bedroom – a mess
- Planet Zelda – home of the Empress – lots of robots

Answers

Page 37

This is just an example of what your plan might look like:

- Sharnie and Mikey are playing on the computer
- Sharnie chooses a new option
- Flash! They find themselves on the planet Zelda
- The Empress captures them
- Sharnie uses her knowledge of the game to help them escape
- They use the Empress's computer to get back to the bedroom
- They decide not to play that game again!

Page 38

A new paragraph should have been started at the phrase: 'Up in the loft… ' (This marks a movement in setting and time.)

Page 39

These are examples of how you might start the story:

- (Description) The screen on the computer lit up with the vivid landscape of the planet Zelda.
- (Action) Zap! Another laser blast struck its target.
- (Dialogue) 'Come on Sharnie, let me have a go,' whined Mikey.

Page 40

These are examples of sentences showing the character of Jess:

- (Appearance) Jess always looked immaculate – her hair, her clothes, even her nails were perfect.
- (Bossy) Jess entered the room and immediately switched over to her favourite channel.

Page 41

These are examples of details you could feed into your story:

- aisles blocked with people and trolleys
- a wall of baked bean tins
- annoying music
- special offer signs in neon colours
- queues of grumbling shoppers at the checkouts…

Page 42

This is an example of a last line for the story:

I'm all for realistic adventures – but that had been just a little too real.

Page 43

Here are two examples:

1 A vast, ultra-modern residence
2 A tiny ramshackle cottage

Page 44

Here is an example of a dialogue for this situation:

'What's that?' asked Sheena.

'It's a key. I found it in that bag of rubbish. It looks very old,' replied Tarik.

'Well a key's not much use. Throw it away,' grumbled Sheena, grabbing an armful of rubbish.

'But it might belong to something in that bag,' said Tarik thoughtfully.

Page 45

Kris heard someone call his name. 'Chaz! Chaz! Is that you? Where are you?' Kris shouted.

'I'm over here, behind the fireplace. There's some sort of secret tunnel,' said the voice.

'How did you get in there?' asked Kris,…

Page 46

This is an example of how you might build up the tension:

Two buttons – one red, one blue. Which one should she choose? One would get them home safely, but if she chose the wrong one… who knows what might happen? Red or blue? What a decision to have to make.

Page 47

This is an example of how you might have used these techniques:

Flash! There was a startling blaze of light. What was happening? Sam could see nothing. Had she pressed the wrong button? She gripped her brother's hand tightly. She could feel him trembling next to her…

Page 48

This is an example of how Luke might reply:

Luke: Just give me a second. He must have put the note in this desk. I must find out what it said.

Page 49

Form – leaflet
Purpose – to inform and persuade
Audience – parents

Page 50

Your introduction should be something like this:

The members of Class 6 are organising a campaign for the collection and recycling of waste material. We believe that recycling is of vital importance for the future of the world and we would like you to join us in our campaign. This leaflet will help answer your questions about recycling and show you why it is so important.

Your conclusion might be something like this:

Remember, recycling helps to save the world's natural resources. So, with your help, we really can save the world!

Answers

Page 51
This is an example of what your plan might look like:
Introduction – purpose of report; describe local area
1 Sports facilities – describe what is available
2 Sports facilities – what is needed
3 Entertainment facilities – what is available
4 Entertainment facilities – what is needed
5 Parks, playgrounds – what is available
6 Parks, playgrounds – what is needed
7 Interests of young people – new ideas
Conclusion – overall comments, ideas for the future

Page 52
This is an example of how you might develop ideas in the paragraph:
There were paper bags floating in the paddling pool and drink cans lying on the grass. The bins were overflowing. They obviously had not been emptied for some time.
In contrast, I would like to praise the particularly helpful member of staff who runs the refreshments kiosk next to the playground…

Page 53
Your topic sentences should be something like these:
1 The farm was set up in 2003 so that children from the city could experience farm life and caring for animals.
2 The farm is now a popular attraction in the local area, and it plans to organise residential visits for schools in the future.
3 There are many things for you to do on your visit.
4 We would like to remind visitors that this is a working farm.

Page 54
• Bullet point list of items needed
• Sub-headings for the different stages
• Numbered points
• Diagram to help explain what to do.

Page 55
1 Your address and the date – top right
2 Dear ___/Hi there
3 See you soon/Best wishes/Take care

Page 56
A possible example might be:
New Kick-Start trainers – the coolest on the block!

Page 57
A more formal version might be:
The council is planning to replace the traditional school crossing patrol with a modern pelican crossing. This decision has caused some debate, and many people do not approve of the idea.

Page 58
1 Take the first turning on the left.
2 Check the cake after 30 minutes. Make sure it is golden brown.

Page 59
The diary entry should open something like this:
Thursday, July 30th (8.30 p.m.) –
What an absolutely brilliant day! We're just back from Alton Towers (me, mum, dad and Tony – unfortunately).

Page 60
Something like: Forest fires continued to burn yesterday in many areas of southern Spain.

Page 61
Possible sub-headings for the report are:
• Games and entertainment
• Finding information
• Presenting work
• Keeping in touch
• Designing and composing…

Page 62
A more persuasive example might be:
Obviously, a mobile phone is absolutely essential for letting worried parents know when you are going to be late home.

Page 63
The next paragraph should begin something like this:
However, local shopkeepers are worried that fewer visitors in the town centre will mean less business for them.

Page 64
Work on your weakest areas as suggested.

Page 65
Possible examples:
1 The frightened child walked down the busy street.
2 The exhausted children came to a neat little cottage with a blue door.
3 The wise old sailor watched the stormy sea.

Page 66
carefully, quietly

Page 67
Ali put the hat on. It was too big and fell over his eyes. This can't be mine thought Ali. It must be Ed's.

Page 68
However

Answers

Page 69
Possible examples:
1 He missed the bus but another one came straightaway.
2 She shouted and shouted and eventually someone came.

Page 70
Here are some examples:
- (Question) What's your favourite flavour?
- (Command) Taste the real fruit.
- (Exclamation) Totally delicious!

Page 71
although

Page 72
Possible sentences might be:
1 Despite her fears, she stepped onto the stage.
2 Relieved that they were gone, he climbed down.

Page 73
The dog, barking madly, was desperate to escape.

Page 74
Dad was not pleased. Well, would you be? He'd been stuck in the house all day looking after a sick cat. Angry? He was positively fuming!

Page 75
Many people keep animals as pets. Cats and dogs are particularly popular. Other people prefer smaller animals, such as gerbils or hamsters.

Page 76
1 Mr Roberts, my teacher, is very strange.
2 First, sieve the flour into the bowl.
3 Although it was very late, we were wide awake.

Page 77
1 He made it to the bus stop – just as the bus pulled out.
2 For dinner there was shepherd's pie (yuk!) and sprouts (double yuk).

Page 78
1 Then the announcement came: 'We regret that this flight is cancelled'.
2 The door opened; a strange man peered at me.

Page 79
Check your spellings in a dictionary.

Page 80
1 des/per/ate
2 fam/i/ly
3 pre/dict

Page 81
1 beautiful
2 heavier
3 arrival
4 dishonest
5 immature
6 uncomfortable

Page 82
1 worried, worrying
2 smiled, smiling
3 hummed, humming
4 screamed, screaming

Page 83
1 squirrel
2 deprive
3 belief

Page 84
1 savage
2 ceiling
3 cinema
4 solid
5 cylinder

Page 85
1 blew
2 brake
3 serial

Page 86
Follow the instructions on page 86.

Curriculum chart

Primary National Strategy – Framework for literacy, Years 5 and 6

Revision Guide

Word structure and spelling	Topic	Pages
Spell words containing unstressed vowels (Year 5)	Breaking words into syllables	80
Know and use less common prefixes and suffixes (Year 5)	Root words, prefixes and suffixes	81
Group and classify words according to spelling patterns (Year 5)	Verb and plural endings; More spelling rules; Difficult letters	82, 83, 84
Spell familiar words correctly and employ a range of strategies to spell difficult and unfamiliar words (Year 6)	Learning to spell; Breaking words into syllables	79, 80
Use a range of appropriate strategies to edit, proofread and correct spelling in their own work (Year 6)	[Complete spelling section]	79–85

Understanding and interpreting texts	Topic	Pages
Make notes on and use evidence from across a text to explain events or ideas (Year 5)	Finding information; Inferring – looking for clues	24, 25, 26
Infer writers' perspectives from what is written and from what is implied (Year 5)	Characters; The fiction author's point of view; The non-fiction author's point of view; The non-fiction author's methods	6, 7, 9, 30, 32
Compare different types of narrative and information texts and identify how they are structured (Year 5)	Following the plot; Genre – type of story; The non-fiction author's purpose; How non-fiction texts are presented	5, 12, 27, 28
Explore how writers use language for comic and dramatic effects (Year 5)	The fiction author's methods; The fiction author's choice of language; The poet's choice of language; Sound patterns	8, 10, 11, 18, 19, 20
Appraise a text quickly, deciding on its value, quality or usefulness (Year 6)	Reading non-fiction	23
Understand underlying themes, causes and points of view (Year 6)	The fiction author's point of view; Themes and messages; The non-fiction author's point of view; Sources and opinions	9, 13, 30, 31
Understand how writers use different structures to create coherence and impact (Year 6)	Following the plot; Poem structure and form	5, 21
Explore how word meanings change when used in different Contexts (Year 6)	Homophones and other tricky words	85
Recognise rhetorical devices used to argue, persuade, mislead and sway the reader (Year 6)	The non-fiction author's point of view; The non-fiction author's methods	30, 32

Engaging with and responding to texts	Topic	Pages
Compare the usefulness of techniques such as visualisation, prediction and empathy in exploring the meaning of texts (Year 5)	How to read a story; Reading poems; Responding to poems	4, 16, 17
Read extensively and discuss personal reading with others, including in reading groups (Year 6)	Responding to fiction; Responding to poems; Writing a commentary; Responding to non-fiction	15, 17, 22, 33

Curriculum chart

Primary National Strategy – Framework for literacy, Years 5 and 6

Revision Guide

Creating and shaping texts	Topic	Pages
Adapt non-narrative forms and styles to write fiction or factual texts, including poems (Year 5)	Writing different text types	58, 59, 60, 61, 62, 63
Vary the pace and develop the viewpoint through the use of direct and reported speech, portrayal of action and selection of detail (Year 5)	Using dialogue; Style in fiction	44, 45, 46, 47
Reflect independently and critically on their own writing and edit and improve it (Year 6)	A checklist for writing	64
Experiment with different narrative forms and styles to write their own stories (Year 6)	Developing ideas; Writing a script;	35, 48
Set their own challenges to extend achievement and experience in writing (Year 6)	Writing stories – starting points; Non-fiction writing – the task	34, 49
Use different narrative techniques to engage and entertain the reader (Year 6)	Interesting openings; Developing characters; Developing settings; Effective endings	39, 40, 41, 42
In non-narrative, establish, balance and maintain viewpoints (Year 6)	Writing different text types	62, 63
Select words and language drawing on their knowledge of literary features and formal and informal writing (Year 6)	Using description; The audience – formal or informal? Formal writing	43, 56, 57

Text structure and organisation	Topic	Pages
Experiment with the order of sections and paragraphs to achieve different effects (Year 5)	Using paragraphs in non-fiction	52
Change the order of material within a paragraph, moving the topic sentence (Year 5)	Using paragraphs in non-fiction	53
Use varied structures to shape and organise text coherently (Year 6)	Planning a story; Plotting events; Using paragraphs in non-fiction; Introductions and conclusions; Planning – organising your ideas; Setting out your writing	36, 37, 38, 50, 51, 54
Use paragraphs to achieve pace and emphasis (Year 6)	Using paragraphs in fiction; Using paragraphs in non-fiction	38, 52, 53

Sentence structure and punctuation	Topic	Pages
Adapt sentence construction to different text types, purposes and readers (Year 5)	Writing in sentences; Sentence types; Complex sentences	69, 70, 71
Punctuate sentences accurately, including using speech marks and apostrophes (Year 5)	Punctuation; Sentence punctuation	74, 75
Express subtle distinctions of meaning, including hypothesis, speculation and supposition, by constructing sentences in varied ways (Year 6)	Complex sentences	72, 73
Use punctuation to clarify meaning in complex sentences (Year 6)	Commas; Dashes and brackets; Colons and semi-colons	76, 77, 78

Glossary

action	an event that happens in a story or play
active	in an active sentence, the subject of the sentence performs the action (e.g., in 'Mark paid the fine.' the subject of the sentence is Mark – he paid the fine) (compare to passive)
adverb	a word that describes or adds to a verb or sentence, giving extra information about what is happening – such as how, when or where an event takes place (e.g., 'He paid the fine reluctantly')
alliteration	a sound effect created when a series of words, placed close together, all begin with the same letter sound (e.g., 'furiously flinging flans')
clause	the part of a sentence containing a verb – a clause can form a complete sentence, or be part of a longer sentence
connective	a word or phrase that links different parts of text (e.g. finally, however, just then)
consonant	apart from the five vowels, all of the other letters in the alphabet are consonants
description	a written account that creates for the reader a picture of a person, place, object or event
dialogue	a conversation between two or more people or characters
fable	a traditional story with a moral or message – the main characters are usually animals
fact	something that is generally accepted to be true – there should be clear evidence to support a fact (compare to opinion)
figurative language	language that describes something in terms of something else (e.g., 'icicles glinted through the darkness like spikes of broken glass') – simile and metaphor are types of figurative language
genre	a word used to describe different kinds of writing
imperative	a type of sentence that gives an order or an instruction (e.g., 'Put that plate back!')
infer	draw out ideas from the information given
key words	the most important words in a sentence – key words are used to help locate information and in note-making
metaphor	a form of image where the writer compares the subject with something else – rather than saying it is 'like' something else (see simile), a metaphor uses no linking word
mnemonic	a trick to help you remember something – it might be a saying, a rhyme, or a chant
narrator	the person telling a story – either a character in the story (first person narration), or someone watching the events (third person narration)
narration	the telling of the story (see narrator)
noun	a word that names something or someone (e.g., girl, gentleman, table, pencil)
onomatopoeia	words that make the same sound as the noise they are describing (e.g., 'splash', 'hiss', 'splat')

Glossary

opinion	an idea, belief or point of view held by some people, but one that cannot be proved definitely true (compare to fact)
passive	a passive sentence is the opposite of an active one, e.g., 'The fine was paid (by Mark)'. The subject of the sentence is the fine, which is passive, as it does nothing. Instead the action of paying happens to it. The person who did the action (Mark) might not be included in the sentence at all
person	this refers to first, second or third person: • first person – the writer refers to himself or herself (I, we) • second person – the writer refers to the reader (you) • third person – the writer refers to someone else (he, she, they)
personification	a description of something as if it were human, e.g., giving it human feelings, actions or thoughts ('Night crept up on us')
plan	the first stage in the writing process – it involves gathering together and ordering ideas, usually in note form
plot	the chain of events in a story, with all the events linked together leading to the end of the story
point of view	this can refer to either a viewpoint (e.g., someone through whose eyes a story is told) or an opinion or position taken on a particular subject (e.g., a non-fiction writer might hold a particular point of view on their subject)
pronoun	a word used in place of a noun (e.g., him, her, it)
proof reading	a final check of a piece of writing, usually checking for punctuation and spelling errors
quotation	words taken directly from a person or text (a 'quote' is short for 'quotation' and means the same thing)
root word	a word that can have prefixes or suffixes added to it to make new words (e.g., the root word 'happy' can be made into 'unhappy', 'happiness', 'happily'…)
scan	to quickly look over a text, trying to find a particular key word rather than reading it fully
simile	a form of image where the writer compares the subject with something else, using the words 'like' or 'as' to make the comparison (e.g., 'Yasmin runs like the wind; she is as fast as a cheetah') (compare with metaphor)
skim	to look through a text to get a rough idea of the content or organisation
syllable	part of a word – some words are only one syllable long (e.g., dog), longer words can be broken down into a number of syllables (e.g., pow/er/ful)
techniques	the methods that authors use to make their writing work well – different authors usually have different techniques
verb	a 'doing' or 'being' word (e.g., 'Adrian was cold. He shivered.')
vowel	any one of the five letters a, e, i, o, or u

Index